THE "BRITISH HERITAGE" SERIES
Uniform with this Volume

PREHISTORIC ENGLAND
By GRAHAME CLARK

THE GREATER ENGLISH
CHURCH
By HARRY BATSFORD and
CHARLES FRY

THE CATHEDRALS OF
ENGLAND
By HARRY BATSFORD and
CHARLES FRY

THE PARISH CHURCHES
OF ENGLAND
By J. CHARLES COX and
C. BRADLEY FORD

THE ENGLISH ABBEY
By F. H. CROSSLEY

THE ENGLISH CASTLE
By HUGH BRAUN

THE ENGLISH COUNTRY
HOUSE
By RALPH DUTTON

THE ENGLISH GARDEN
By RALPH DUTTON

THE ENGLISH COTTAGE
By HARRY BATSFORD and
CHARLES FRY

ENGLISH VILLAGES AND
HAMLETS
By HUMPHREY PAKINGTON

ENGLISH VILLAGE HOMES
By SYDNEY R. JONES

THE OLD TOWNS OF
ENGLAND
By CLIVE ROUSE

THE OLD INNS OF
ENGLAND
By A. E. RICHARDSON

THE OLD PUBLIC SCHOOLS
OF ENGLAND
By JOHN RODGERS

THE HEART OF ENGLAND
By IVOR BROWN

THE COUNTRYMAN'S
ENGLAND
By DOROTHY HARTLEY

OLD ENGLISH
HOUSEHOLD LIFE
By GERTRUDE JEKYLL and
SYDNEY R. JONES

OLD ENGLISH CUSTOMS
AND CEREMONIES
By F. J. DRAKE-CARNELL

THE SEAS AND SHORES
OF ENGLAND
By EDMUND VALE

THE SPIRIT OF LONDON
By PAUL COHEN-PORTHEIM

THE FACE OF SCOTLAND
By HARRY BATSFORD and
CHARLES FRY

THE HEART OF SCOTLAND
By GEORGE BLAKE

THE LAND OF WALES
By EILUNED and PETER LEWIS

THE SPIRIT OF IRELAND
By LYNN DOYLE

Published by
B. T. BATSFORD LTD.
15 North Audley Street, London, W.1
and Malvern Wells, Worcestershire

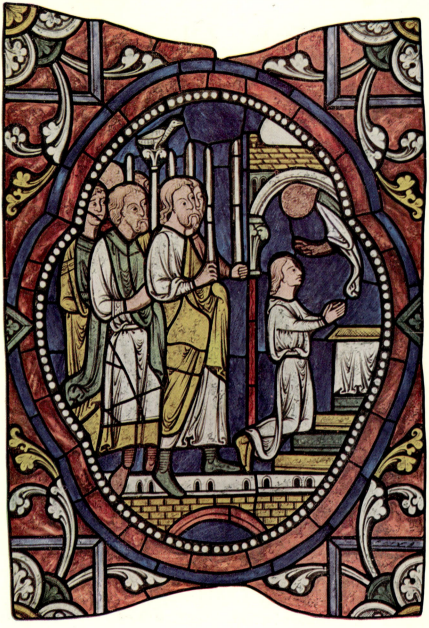

1. A ROUNDEL OF EARLY THIRTEENTH-CENTURY GLASS, LINCOLN CATHEDRAL
SUBJECT PROBABLY THE DEDICATION OF ST. HUGH

From a watercolour by Charles Winston in the British Museum

English Church Craftsmanship

AN INTRODUCTION TO THE WORK OF THE MEDIAEVAL PERIOD AND SOME ACCOUNT OF LATER DEVELOPMENTS

by

FRED H. CROSSLEY, F.S.A.

Author of "*English Church Monuments*," "*The English Abbey*," &c.

Illustrated by Photographs by the Author & others

LONDON: B. T. BATSFORD LTD.
15 NORTH AUDLEY STREET, MAYFAIR
& MALVERN WELLS, WORCESTERSHIRE

First Published, Spring 1941

*The corbel on the title-page is from the
nave of St. Mary's Beverley, Yorkshire*

MADE AND PRINTED IN GREAT BRITAIN
FOR THE PUBLISHERS B. T. BATSFORD LTD.
LONDON AND MALVERN WELLS
BY UNWIN BROTHERS LTD., WOKING

PREFACE

THIS little book, though long considered, was not written until the modern Hun was destroying the English heritage of craftsmanship, our treasure-house of the work of our forefathers connecting our history with the past, work irreparably lost, which cannot be replaced, and must now join that consummated by the Suppression and the Civil Wars. In this supposed age of civilisation it had not been thought possible that there should still exist a people whose mind was sufficiently warped and twisted as to be capable of such savage barbarism; but the Nordic blood which produced the original Hun still carries with it the seeds of degeneration and destruction that have again broken out in a still more virulent form, and with further disastrous results. Within the cover of this book is gathered a fraction of the England we once knew, a side not always before the public, but as essential to a knowledge of the origins of our present status as many more loudly proclaimed assets. It may with truth be called "A Glory that was England."

FRED H. CROSSLEY

19 SHAVINGTON AVENUE, CHESTER
Spring 1941

ACKNOWLEDGMENT

THE selection of the illustrations has been made with much thought from something like 10,000 subjects, with the definite end in mind of illustrating craftsmanship and its design; the antiquarian side of church features and furniture has been deliberately excluded from its scope, for it has already appeared in several volumes dealing with the more archaelogical side of the church.

There are as we know to our cost many hundreds of examples crying aloud for inclusion in a volume on craftsmanship, but it is impossible to produce a 21s. book for 8s. 6d., and although at times the selection may seem inadequate or arbitrary, we do claim to have brought together a collection of pictures of church craftsmanship in a manner not essayed before, in which there has been an endeavour to hold the balance between the various divisions; to satisfy every taste is, however, an impossibility.

If a number of English folk are, as a result, enabled to appreciate something of their national heritage in church craftsmanship, and will take the trouble to seek it out and help to preserve it, our intention will have been achieved. We have enough material for a second series of equal interest and merit to this; indeed for a whole range of successors devoted one by one to each varied material. It is for the public to say whether they would like to see recorded more of what wealth English churches still possess, before this is jeopardised or destroyed.

We should ourselves have liked to include a far larger selection of Renaissance subjects from the post-Reformation period: this would however have involved an even more imperfect presentation of the types of mediaeval work. A fine volume could be produced on this later work extending over nearly three centuries; we should love to do it, and there is no difficulty in its compilation or production, but the indications are definitely that the popular interest is so restricted that it would prove commercially and financially unsuccessful.

The majority of the illustrations are reproduced from the author's photographs; a number are by the late Brian C. Clayton, and from other sources in the publishers' collection. We must in addition thank the following photographers and authors who have kindly contributed: Mr. Arthur Gardner, F.S.A., Fig. 66; the Rev. Chancellor Harrison, York, Fig. 118; Mr. A. F. Kersting, F.R.P.S., Battersea, London, Figs. 47, 82, 92, 93, 167; Mr. Sidney Pitcher, F.R.P.S., Gloucester, Figs. 55, 123, 157; the late Mr. S. Smith, Lincoln, Fig. 56; the Victoria and Albert Museum, Fig. 11; Fig. 131 is from a drawing by Professor Tristram and was published in Dr. Tancred Borenius's *English Painting of the Middle Ages* in the *Pegasus* series; of the coloured plates the frontispiece (Fig. 1) is reproduced by kind permission of the British Museum from a drawing by Charles Winston; Figs. 132 and 133 are by arrangement with Messrs. John Lane Ltd. from Kendon's *Mural Paintings in English Churches during the Middle Ages.*

F. H. C.

B. T. B. LTD.

DEDICATION

CONTENTS

2 DEVIZES, ST. JOHN, EAST END OF SOUTH AISLE

3 SALISBURY CATHEDRAL, CHAPTER-HOUSE

ENGLISH CHURCH CRAFTSMANSHIP

INTRODUCTION

In early mediaeval times the spirit of architecture and the arts as practised in Northern Europe differed essentially from the sunny materialistic outlook of the South. For more than half the year it was a land of brooding mist and fog, storm and tempest, lit by the pale rays of the sun; a land producing saints and mystics, rugged and rock-girt, craggy and inclement, the north wind moaning through the dark mountain forests. The imagination of the builders was tinged with the mood, and they erected churches, bastioned out, boldly projected, fretted by the elements into jagged heights. The interiors were shadowy, the high vaults shrouded in gloom, illuminated by the stray gleams of sunlight filtering through high and narrow windows. The art of the time seems touched by some eerie imagination, humour when it breaks through is a little grim and macabre; it was a time of belief in devils as well as saints, the former appealing to the romantic and illusionary mind of the time.

In England this outlook was softened and domesticated, more homely and attractive, in fact less bizarre. Our churches contain no such flights of imagination, nor did they soar into the ether as did those of the Continent, but stayed sane and manageable in their proportions. As the centuries passed, the love of light and sunshine was surely reflected in the breadth of window and the absence of gloom; this attitude, more comfortable to both the mind and well-being of a people, was shown also in their love of colour, and the dainty invention of much of their carving and ornament. Devils were driven outside, their only foothold the parapets of the church, clinging in precarious postures, acting the part of gargoyles spewing water from the roofs (137), while inside angels took their place, nestling on the roof-timbers (153), or attending deceased knights and their ladies during long vigils (81).

Nevertheless a solicitude for the souls of the deceased tinged the mind and formed an essential element of the people's worship, which was reflected also in the decoration of their churches. The masses for the dead and the lovely tombs and chantry chapels point to the importance of this belief; a future existence with its problems of place and position in an ethereal state largely controlled the benevolence of the worshippers, who endeavoured to engage thereby the interest and pity of their patron saints to intercede on their behalf; there remained however a core of bargaining, to accompany this belief which did not prevent folk from living a rather graceless existence, trusting that the saints in their purity and pity would sponge away their record or mitigate their sentence.

This predilection to brood upon the future state took on many forms; in the earlier centuries men joined together in communities shut away from the world, devoting themselves to the worship of God and the intercession of his saints, that by continual prayer and praise they might find favour in his sight, and be permitted to enjoy their share in the heavenly mansions. To this end, and for their use, many glorious churches were erected, which in course of time became enriched with the finest work that craftsmanship could produce. The majority of these monastic buildings were destroyed at the suppression and the remainder looted, and we can therefore only surmise about their contents and the gracious beauty they exhibited. At a later date and in the same way the chantry chapels, endowed for the benefit of the souls of the donors, their families and ancestors, were filled with treasures of craftsmanship. It is to this operative desire for the welfare of the soul that we owe the religious architecture and the craftsmanship of the mediaeval period, and it is to the latter subject particularly that attention will be drawn in the following pages.

The incubation of mediaeval craftsmanship was of long duration and the times remote, broken by short oases of high artistic effort in a desert of the crude and immature, blossoming out in such admirable productions as the crosses at Bewcastle and Ruthwell and the marvellous illuminated manuscripts of the book of Kells; but constant invasions, internecine wars, unsettled governments and the deadly quarrels over religious questions effectively repressed artistic expression, and caused the crafts to wait for their expansion until a later age.

Although the Norman invasion brought about a settled form of government, and a homogeneous religion, the vindictiveness and waste involved to the country in the effort made for supremacy suppressed artistic endeavour. The energies of the victors were taken up in the erection of great fortress churches, stark, frowning and grim, devoid of ornament and destitute of grace in which the gentler arts found no place. When, later, decoration in stone was attempted it was cut with a hatchet, and was confined to simple patterns surrounding doorways or arches into sanctuaries. The few strivings made to depict the human figure were rudimentary and untrained. However, by the commencement of the twelfth century, with the settlement of monastic communities in their new homes, desire sprang up to furnish the churches with some degree of order and beauty.

The more cultivated among clerics and nobles sought for talent where it could be found, either within or without the convent walls; craftsmanship was fostered and encouraged, and the foundations laid for the progression of the arts which was to last for nearly four hundred years. During the whole of this time craftsmen were under the patronage of ecclesiastics and the king. Art was fostered by the church for the church, primarily for the enrichment of the House of God. Before the suppression the churches had gathered into their possession the finest craftsmanship produced during the mediaeval period, the accumulation of centuries of intelligent devotion, and this in spite of pestilence, devastating wars and royal and ecclesiastical cupidity.

From the twelfth century onwards architecture had a continuous development, especially in the scientific use of materials. Fostered by the stress of some economic urge, there was a consistent striving to improve construction and minimise the weight of material. These efforts were principally directed towards solving the difficult problem of throwing a vault of stone over an uneven space keeping at the same time an even keel. The solution was eventually found in the pointed arch, and, from its use as a constructional expedient, it was later developed as a decorative feature, becoming the main factor in what has been called "Gothic architecture." In the same way towards the close of the fourteenth century, the continued scourge of the Black Death was responsible for the so-called "Perpendicular" style. The men of the Severn Valley, who had been largely immune, were encouraged to travel and work in other centres, taking with them their local and individual methods of treating current architecture, shown first at St. Augustine's, Bristol, and later in the south transept at Gloucester. This style revolutionised masons' procedure, for the carving and cutting could now be executed either at the quarry centres or in the gild shops, instead of being worked on the site of the building. This gradually altered the status of both mason and shopman, causing them to change places, the gild men becoming the more important partners.

After the suppression interest in mediaeval architecture dwindled and finally became extinct, and it was not until the close of the eighteenth century that tentative studies of what was termed "Gothic" (given in contempt) made any headway, to gather certainly in force during the following century. The early adventurers into the style roughly divided the period into sections, each given its appropriate tag or whatever, such as Early-English or Lancet, Decorated or Middle Pointed, again divided into Geometrical, Curvilinear or Flowing, Flamboyant, and finally Perpendicular, each name culled from some feature seized upon to denote its type. This though vastly convenient had its disadvantages, for it is impossible to place a finger upon any particular date and say that at this moment the alteration to a particular style took place. Dates for one district bear little relation to another, for the time-lag varied considerably, and at no time did one type supersede another with the click of precision, but came as the outcome of experiment, often the result of topographical conditions, which, catching the eye of an advanced patron or his "Magister Operandi," was used on some important building and thus became stylised.

The elements employed by the craftsmen for the enrichment of the churches were remarkably few in number, but surprisingly adequate for the work they were called upon to perform, and their rendering was so perfectly understood that they rarely became monotonous or wearisome. The same handful of ideas was used again and again in stone, timber, glass, metal, tiles and other materials, bringing out the special qualities in each, and showing a fresh aspect of the design. These elements may be divided into three types: architectural, natural and abstract forms, and it is only in the second that we ever catch the crafts-man astray. The units comprising the first class consist of rounds and hollows applied to mouldings, shafts and tracery enriched with cusps, crockets and finials, and with these few ideas was produced that infinite variety which is called "Gothic."

The architectural elements were taken directly from the construction of the building and adapted to ornamental pur-poses in its decoration. To take the forms of capital, vaulting rib and tracery; these were used with magnificent effect as the principal ingredients of a splendid cathedral such as Exeter; they were also applied with equal success to a small niche. The gable is as much at home in the termination of a great abbey, the finish to a canopied tomb, or the decoration of a small piscina. Tracery was used to fill the great west window of York cathedral, as it was to decorate the small panels in front of the desks of the singing boys within the Minster. The buttresses and pinnacles were brought from the exterior and requisitioned for this new purpose, reproduced in miniature, and made entirely relevant to their new positions. There is no question as to the fun the craftsmen got out of the job of adapting these elements to their designs, whether it be reredos or sedilia, metalwork or wooden stalls; as Lethaby so poetically noted "the folk had fallen in love with building, some of their

4 ELY CATHEDRAL, BISHOP WEST'S CHANTRY

5 CANTERBURY CATHEDRAL, STONE PULPITUM

6 BEVERLEY MINSTER, NORTH SIDE OF PERCY TOMB

7 OXFORD, QUIRE VAULT OF ST. FRIDESWIDE'S, NOW THE CATHEDRAL

tombs and shrines must have been conceived as little fairy buildings; they would have liked little angels to hop about them all alive and blowing fairy trumpets." The outstanding elements of the later time were nichework and canopies, forming as they did the principal contribution of all designs for tombs, stallwork, sanctuary fittings and the like. They were used externally, flanking doorways, decorating buttresses and towers, and within, wherever the statue of a saint was thought desirable; they are the glory of the splendid tabernacled stalls; they grace the fronts of pulpitums and galleries of screens, such lovely things as the Neville reredos at Durham and the sedilia at Exeter; they protect the effigies lying upon the chest tombs with spectacular canopies, as that over the Percy tomb at Beverley (6, 169), and they decorate the sides of the tomb with continuous nichework. They appear in golden richness in the fourteenth and fifteenth century glass panels, towering above the saints they glorify, and in Yorkshire they are peopled with little angels blowing silver trumpets.

The second type was inspired by a study of nature, including foliage, flower and insect forms, occasionally animals, and much figurework, now unhappily almost exterminated. I say inspired by nature advisedly, for with the exception of about thirty years at the turn of the thirteenth and fourteenth centuries there was little direct copying of nature, though during that short span the craftsmen had shown with what delight they could produce a close study of what they saw around them. In Southwell chapter-house this fills us with wondering admiration (44), but we prefer the carver when he uses nature only for inspiration for his architectural conventions, be they early trefoil or the later squared foliage, whose undulating surfaces give such a charming variety of light and shade. From the early twelfth century we may watch the craftsmen's gradual evolution of foliage; the kernel of this mediaeval format is found in the rough shell of Norman, and it is of the greatest interest to examine the multitudinous examples of its early sproutings and tentative growth, before it crystallised into the conventional lily form of the early thirteenth century. Before the close of that century there was that short season of natural growth, suggesting a rapid spring of lovely flowering, which however, soon turned into an architectural rendering of foliage. By the middle of the fourteenth century commenced the long summer of what Rickman terms his "Perpendicular" period. With the passage of time it perhaps grew a little dusty and stale, the decoration a little stiff and stereotyped with long continuance; at the commencement of the sixteenth century however it showed a noble vitality, but was struck down before the cycle was completed by the frost of circumstance. We have moreover lost many valuable links in the chain owing to that voracious monarch Henry VIII, who was more intrigued by matrimonial agencies than architectural continuities. Under his rule many hundreds of fine churches suffered eclipse together with their contents, to the loss of many aspects which would have enabled us to develop the tale of our architectural progression. Lastly, there was the craftsmen's use of abstract forms such as lettering, monograms, badges and coats of arms, giving his latent love of pure colour the chance to blazon window, vault and tomb with a mosaic of jewelled brightness.

At no time did the craftsmen however keep to the rigid copy of the proportions of nature; their ideas of proportions were of two kinds, architectural and symbolic. In the architectural, the figure sculpture which filled the façades and porches of the great religious buildings was governed by the aspirations of the time in which it was executed. From 1160 to 1260 the outlook was towards slenderness and height, the niches and sculpture partaking of this quality, the figurework delicate and attenuated, but of infinite grace; from 1260 to 1360 the trend was towards breadth and solidity. In the fifteenth century, however, the sculpture lacks the grace of the earlier periods, being inserted into its architectural setting rather than a part of it. In the same way the carvings of birds and beasts are of sufficient size to justify their existence amongst the leafage of boss and corbel when seen from a distance.

Symbolic proportions were governed by the relative importance of the person or object portrayed; the donor of a window or reredos was often shown as a diminutive figure kneeling beside his patron saint, just as the patron saint of an abbey was depicted holding a small model of his church in his hand. The more important the saint the larger his representation became; Saint Christopher, a popular saint in Yorkshire, is usually painted at least seven feet in height. The same thought is carried through the memorials, the animal at the feet of the knight and the angels guarding the pillows of his lady being miniatures, as were the figures of the relatives or weepers surrounding the tomb. Heart burials, or children are carved as a miniature of an adult, placed upon corresponding tombs. This mingling of the greater and the lesser figure in the same composition is often most attractive, and the craftsmen did not fail to turn this to account. Symbolism like heraldry grew to be of much importance in mediaeval art; the many figures of the saints are distinguished by their appropriate symbols, which they either carried, or had reproduced as a shield or arms above or even in place of them.

Humour took several forms, the grotesque, fabulous monsters, birds and reptiles, mermaids and men, centaurs and the like. The brackets or baberies under the seats of stallwork exhibit a series of stories either taken from the natural history books of the time, popular tales, or homely scenes wherein domestic strife was spicily set forth for the benefit of a celibate clergy. The gargoyles on the exterior of churches are often humorous carvings of gesticulating creatures spewing out the rain-water, a devil or monkey assisting by holding open the mouth of the victim. Another form was the punning rebus upon a man's name, which was employed apart from heraldry, especially by the clergy, as at Hereford where pigs disport themselves round the arch above the effigy of dean Swinford. It was this personal touch peeping out upon occasion which gives additional interest to the study of mediaeval art exemplified on two or three monumental brasses where the little pet dogs at the feet of the ladies are named, Bo, at Clifton Reynes, Terrie, at Deerhurst, and Jakke, at Ingham.

In his more intimate moods the craftsmen revealed a sense of humour which to our sophisticated thought suggests grim indecency. We must however bear in mind that the scales of justice were in their day weighted against the accused, and judgment was often given with a grim jesting flippancy, the victim occasionally receiving a sporting chance to add interest to the proceedings of the court. The sense of topsy-turvydom was keen, the mind of the time having much the characteristics of the strong thoughtless schoolboy of today, often inflicting unnecessary suffering upon his juniors. We have also to remember that the greater number of the people were semi-serfs, with the consequent attitude of the rulers that the marketable value of a man was impaired if an injury prevented his usefulness as a soldier or agriculturist; otherwise there was little interference between master and man.

The sources from which the craftsmen derived certain aspects of their representations are sufficiently interesting to merit a passing glance. Throughout the middle ages the love of play-acting was strong, and in spite of later laws and enactments it continued to find an outlet. In the earlier periods this was principally through the mystery plays performed at Whitsuntide, and originally given in the churches by the clergy and their assistants; later they were taken over by the various gilds, each gild being responsible for a mystery, the performances taking place on a wheeled stage drawn up at certain specified places within the jurisdiction of the city. In these dramatic Biblical scenes the carvers found much of their inspiration, as may be noted in the spandrels of the wall-arcading either in the chapter-house at Salisbury (147, 3) or the east end at Worcester. In the mysteries, angels, always men, were clothed in feathered tights leaving the hands and feet bare (155): this is represented in glass in the windows in the south transept at York and in stone on the interior wall of the Beauchamp chapel at Warwick (67), and the Divinity school at Oxford. The carving of the ark at Salisbury is typical of a mystery play, constructed as it is in two storeys with the beasts and birds peeping out of the windows, Noah entering the ark at one end, and sending out the dove from the other (147). The devil, who was regarded in the plays as the clown, dressed in horns, tail and hairy skin, is shown in a piece of glass at York from a figure of a Doom; he is also carved in stone on a corbel at Westwood, Somerset.

What do we know, it may be asked, of the men who produced this richness, this luxury to the eye, this pride of life in their work? In mind and habit the mediaeval craftsman was the child of long continued tradition, which was nevertheless living and progressive; he was unspoilt by a knowledge of other countries and traditions alien to his own (a knowledge we have found to our cost both unsettling to the mind and chaotic to inspiration). He was moreover an iconoclast in his dealings with the experimental work of his forefathers, which he correctly judged to be inferior to his own, and he was anxious to replace with his more scientific and advanced constructional methods when time and opportunity occurred.

Human nature being a fairly constant quantity, it must be understood that the people of the period under review were neither phenomenal nor unusual; they were capable of slipshod work with the worst, though perhaps had more moments of inspiration; they were however fortunate in living at a time when industrialism such as we know it today did not exist, and, being untroubled by wanderlust and the calls of other styles, could devote themselves to improving the traditions they had imbibed. The idealised picture of mediaeval times drawn out by a poetic mind such as that of William Morris has little relation to actuality; it was produced by his disgust with the self-centred, self-satisfied, industrialised and sordid world in which he found himself, and which he strove in vain to inform and reform. His idealised version should be set against that of Dr. Coulton's caustic commentary, in which he suggests the period to be infinitely worse than the conditions in which we now live. A middle course is advisable; nevertheless what-

8 TOMB OF QUEEN ELEANOR, WESTMINSTER ABBEY

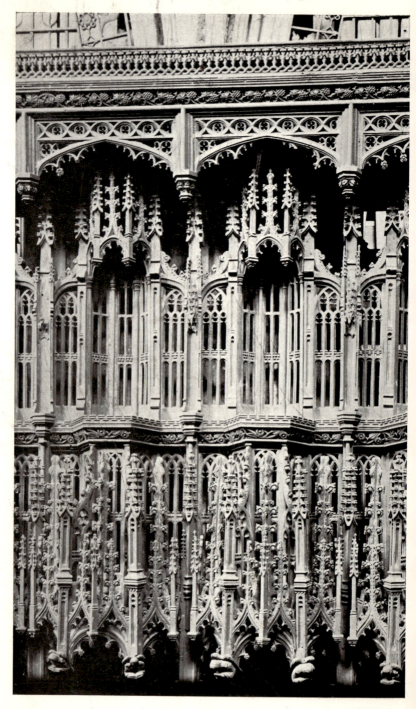

9 MANCHESTER CATHEDRAL, STALLWORK, SOUTH SIDE OF QUIRE

10 LAPFORD SCREEN, DEVONSHIRE

11   CANTERBURY CATHEDRAL, ILLUSTRATING VIRGINITY AND CONTINENCE

ever were the real conditions they produced an atmosphere conducive to a long period of creative and inspired work, an atmosphere for which we now wait in vain, and which under present circumstances can be but a mirage without substance or form. The mind of man in the aggregate much resembles that of a child; first absorbed in the creation of an idea, and, having completed it to his satisfaction, his brother, filled with a spirit of destruction, knocks it down with entire indifference, if not with savage glee; such was the work of the Reformation, and again we are the spectators of a more malevolent and infernal demonstration of the aptitude of the teutonic mind for taking the brother's part.

But to return to the craftsmen: what knowledge do we possess of their actual methods of work, the wages they earned and the position they occupied? Practically nothing, or to qualify, did not until in recent years the various fabric rolls which have been haphazardly preserved came to be studied. Here are many names attached to wage-sheets of the craftsmen of those far-off times, which enables us if only for a moment to drop into the picture and survey the scene, which as quickly eludes our grasp, and we are left fingering these slender threads linking us with the past. Although the personality behind the work is always fascinating, it is after all by the quality of the performance that artists and craftsmen are to be judged. A picture, a book, or a carving, if created by a sensitive brain with a full grasp of the vibrations and meaning of life, will live, though the creator's name be lost and his body mingles with the dust. Better to have given the world a sterling piece of work though nameless, than retain a name of the character of a Thomas Cromwell, à Layton or an Adolf Hitler.

It is then to the quality of the work we must devote our attention, bearing in mind that what we see is but a dim shadow of earlier glories now vanished. What is left indeed needs some qualification, for it has gone through a long period of neglect followed by drastic renewal, and is often false, trimmed into something mechanical and superficial. Although to our tidy notions we prefer that it should be so, it would have been well, if we desired to arrive at the truth, that the mediaeval work should have been left, an irreducible minimum, with the touch of the craftsman's handiwork still upon it. It is difficult to say which of the two states is the worse, the church in the eighteenth century, whitewash covering the mediaeval painting, plain windows still containing scattered fragments of glass and high Georgian pews; or the house swept and garnished, scraped and mangled, vulgar and futile, with pitch-pine fittings, gaudy tiles

C

and garish windows. Both conditions are out of the mediaeval picture, and the work remaining bears little relation to its surroundings.

To gain a picture of its former setting we must endeavour to eliminate the present, and with a tense imagination see our church as it was in the fifteenth century. This happy picture would reveal an interior harmonious in colour, walls, roofs, woodwork and windows blended in pictorial fusion—the chancel divided from the nave by a vaulted screen, having a gallery front painted with the saints, which were supplemented by others in the windows and upon the walls, this scheme of beauty would lead up to a sanctuary where the altar was draped in delicate embroidery, the niches of the reredos filled with silver-gilt and jewelled figures, the chantry chapel opening into the chancel fenced by screens, the windows blazoned with the arms of the deceased knight and his lady, sculptured in repose upon an altar tomb, the sides carved with representations of their patron saints, or diminutive figures of mourning relatives, the whole enriched with colour.

Nowadays colour is divorced from its proper setting and confined to windows, often designed with a fine perversity of taste, whose discordant patches have little relation to their surroundings. When studying the scant harvest of mediaeval work, the present setting should not be allowed to destroy its value, and we should endeavour to eliminate a Puritan training of some centuries in our dislike of colour. The present attempts to reach back by a short cut to the old tradition are not only impossible, but have led to many grievous results, the reason why so many of our churches exhibit such horrid failures and queer oddities of design.

In dealing with the question of mediaeval craftsmanship in the bulk, we are at once confronted with the necessity for discrimination and selection: otherwise like life itself it will only lead to confusion and uncertainty. Not all work produced in the mediaeval or any other period is uniformly good; there are degrees of goodness as there are degrees of badness, even to the state of those damned by mediocrity. There were many inspired artists whose work was full of delicate charm and acute perception, as there were others who, following the fashion of the moment, did so adequately and with judgment, but to whom the epithet inspired could never be given. In the rear of the procession came the ordinary come-day go-day shop craftsman, lacking in insight and without imagination, who copied what was set before him, and through constant repetition, not from the original but the copy of a copy, finished by

12, 13 ST. GEORGE'S, WINDSOR. GRILLE TO THE CHAPEL OF EDWARD IV
LOCK PLATE FROM DOOR AT ST. GEORGE'S, WINDSOR

14 ST. MARGARET PATTENS, LONDON, AND (15, 16) LION AND UNICORN
FROM KNOWLE, WARWICKSHIRE

turning the original design into a meaningless hieroglyphic, as witness the decoration upon the alabaster tombs turned out from the Burton centres in the sixteenth century. Unhappily the wheel of fortune in its turning knows nothing of the blessed word discrimination, but with blind indifference destroys the good with the bad, with however a distinct bias towards the good. It is therefore our duty to select for our-selves, and to note the reaction produced to our period, with the play of interaction between one craft and its material with another. We may then possibly find the truth and renew some glimmering of the unity which existed between them. This is an absolute necessity, if we are to justify our infatuation, and acknowledge the fascination by which mediaeval art and craftsmanship holds us in thrall.

THE CRAFT OF THE STONE CARVER

"Criticism cannot be cold, scientific and objective. One praises the artist one would have liked to be, infinitely grateful that he has expressed one's own feelings. Fortunate the man who can create even a little and believe in what he is doing, for that man can never know what it is to be lonely with the worst kind of loneliness of all groping for something vague that he does not clearly understand."

ARNOLD L. HASKELL

THE stone carver was the essential partner with the mason, whose buildings without his aid would have lacked both interest and charm. The work of the carver in the finer periods was sufficiently restrained in output to give an added value to the plain surfaces of the fabric, and to stress the parts reserved for special treatment, such as the portals and western façades. The decorative scheme for a building, apart from the fittings it housed, was kept within well-defined parts of the church, the richness being restricted of course by the funds available and the tenets of the patrons for whom the work was executed. Porches and doorways were ennobled by sculptured figures set in their housings, to say nothing of the earlier elaboration of decorative mouldings. Windows, apart from their tracery, seldom received further embellishment, although fine effects were produced within by the use of double tracery and ornamental arched tracery, and without by deeply scored weather-mouldings terminating in carved heads often realistic in mien.

The EXTERIOR of the building relied for its general effect upon numerous base-mouldings to wall and buttress, also connecting string-courses, and the completion of façades by traceried parapets bristling with pinnacles and dotted with grotesque gargoyles. A common factor of decoration was nichework placed upon the front edge of buttresses, crowning gables, enriching towers and at certain periods inevitably surrounding the main entrances to the church. A doctrinal and connected scheme was planned in connection with the west front of the church, where statuary of great importance was placed before a great stone screen, which sometimes hid the construction of the church. In the last phase this feature was introduced into the interior at the east ends of the quires of the greater churches; in the earlier time however the figurework was lavished upon the west front, as at Wells (54), Lichfield, Salisbury, Lincoln and Beverley; other gables were enriched when meriting that attention, either owing to their importance or because of the sanctity of their position, as the east and south gables at Melrose, originally the south transept at Chester, the east ends of York and Beverley and many others.

WITHIN the building the same careful selection was followed; in the twelfth century surface decoration was sometimes employed, as in the west transept at Ely, but in the fifteenth century walls were panelled, as seen in the quire and transepts at Gloucester and on the exterior of the towers at the same place, Malvern and Cirencester. The interior wall space below the windows of the aisles was from the first enriched by arcading, either single arched, intersecting or super-imposed, and always effective; it is also to be found in the earlier slypes of conventual establishments, as at Gloucester and formerly at St. Albans. In its later forms it became a canopied arcading ranging round the sides of polygonal chapter-houses, and is also suggested in the triforium designs at Chester, both the abbey and St. John's, Southwark and St. Albans; however its finest manifestation is in the Lady chapel at Ely (23).

The Pier-caps (37–47) show a progression of design from the twelfth to the fourteenth centuries (*v. post*, pp. 26–31), after which time the moulded capital predominated; within this period, however, as is shown elsewhere, the wealth of inventiveness and the execution of design is marvellous, ranging the whole gamut from conventional foliage and animal grotesques to pure naturalism and the portrayal of the human head in great nobility and beauty. The bracket and corbel were utilised by the carver to give an infinite variety of subjects from grave to gay, and many a quiet quip is to be found upon careful examination.

VAULTING as time progressed grew more and more a spider's web of loveliness, delicacy and grace (7), picked out by attractively carved bosses originally coloured and gilt. The boss was capable of every mode of decorative device from the extraordinary groups of figures depicting scenes of religious fervour, through genre to grotesques (69, 71, 72, 74, 135, 141–2). It was also used for the blazoning of the arms of patrons, benefactors and donors of the churches; the series of angels playing musical instruments above the quire at Gloucester (55) are carved with sinuous grace and are appropriate to their position in the vault; it was possible however to descend to the amusing stories shown on the baberies below the seating of the stalls. Interior walls both east and west received enrichment, either panelling or tall canopied niches, which were also placed wherever considered expedient. Spandrels formed a further place for decoration, from the simple diapering of the surface found at Chichester to the magnificent angels sculptured in the triforiums at Westminster abbey (66) and Lincoln cathedral.

In the matter of applied decoration the stone carver was the first man in the field, setting the pace for the other craftsmen, who copied his formulas and adapted them to their own requirements, be it in wood, glass, metal or alabaster. The carver evolved the majority of his ideas from the buildings upon which he worked, using varied architectural units to produce his own particular decorative values, and, apart from figure sculpture and foliage, he scored his greatest successes in this class of work, a combination of columns, caps and bases, arcades and buttresses, nichework and canopies, all of which he used in the designing of tombs, chantries, shrines, reredoses, sedilia and the like. An important principle in the homogeneous nature of mediaeval craftsmanship is found in the fact that the decorative qualities with which the building is adorned are inherent in the structure itself, and have no extraneous commitments which have been grafted onto the original stock and never completely assimilated.

After the Norman invasion, in fact until the commencement of the twelfth century, carving was practically non-existent; the churches were rough and ready, heavy and sombre, and if decorated relied upon red and yellow colouring daubed upon the plastered walls. When ORNAMENT first appears it is cut with a hatchet, crude and childish; however, before the middle of the century the progress made was such that enriched mouldings were as numerous as they were diverse, and when grouped round the head of a doorway gave a scintillating if overloaded patterning. The chevron is usually the foundation of all sets, followed by the lozenge (York St. Mary), embattle (west doorway at Kirkstall), disk (Brayton), chain and cable (Castle Acre and Southwell crossing), beakhead (Adel), this last Norse in character; there is a wonderful series of mouldings to be found in a doorway in the castle at Durham (17). When the churches came to be rebuilt in later ages the twelfth century doorways were often preserved and there are many still scattered over the country. The inner semicircular heads of this period are generally cut in the solid, the typanum carved with symbolic subjects which are lacking in variety and often feeble in execution and design, figure sculpture having little quality before the commencement of the thirteenth century. During the middle

SHOWING THE INFINITE VARIETY OF TWELFTH CENTURY MOULDINGS

18 HEREFORD CATHEDRAL, EAST TRANSEPT

17 DURHAM CASTLE DOORWAY

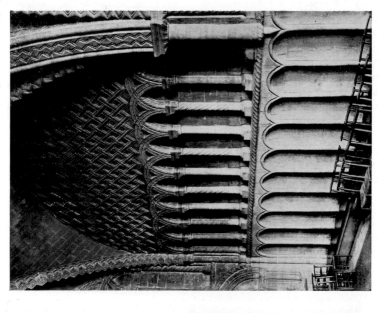

20 BRISTOL, ST. AUGUSTINE'S PRIORY CHAPTER-HOUSE

19 THORNTON ABBEY CHAPTER-HOUSE

of the twelfth century, however, the decoration bestowed upon
portals assumed a magnificence entirely lacking in the earlier
designs, the mouldings now were enriched with medallions
having figure subjects, signs of the zodiac and marvellous
beasts and birds, carved at Brayton and Fishlake in Yorks;
Barfreston (31) and St. Margaret at Cliffe in Kent, Kilpeck in
Herefordshire, at Dunstable, and the superb efforts on the
Glastonbury doorway (49) and the Malmesbury porch, together
with the west doorway at Rochester. Norse influence is evident
at Kilpeck (134, 137) and in both cloister doorways at Ely.

These enriched mouldings were applied to chancel arches and
occasionally for the main arcades as the Galilee at Durham,
Cartmel, Etton, Elkstone, St. Chad Stafford, and later and more
ornate examples are to be found at Broadwater, Castle Acre,
Lichfield and Malmesbury; the chevron was also used for
vaulting ribs as at Bishop's Cleeve. These mouldings found a
home for the rather macabre animals which the early carvers
loved: dragons with crocodile heads terminate the hood
mouldings at Bishop's Cleeve, Bredon, Elkstone (135), Leonard
Stanley and Malmesbury; the same symbolism is seen upon the
corbel tables round many of these twelfth century churches.

Apart from mouldings the principal asset of this period was
the WALL-ARCADE, used indiscriminately for both exterior and
interior decoration: it is carved upon towers, west fronts,
turrets and porches, and inside upon aisle walls, chapter-houses,
porches, slypes, chancels, east-ends and fonts. Simple arcading
is used on the towers of Exeter, Durham, Caistor, Tewkesbury,
the west front of Rochester, and inside the aisles at Ely, New
Shoreham and the Gloucester slype and chapter-house. It is
intersected on the towers of Southwell and Tewkesbury, the
west front of Castle Acre and Castle Rising, and inside in the
aisles of Durham, the quire at Bolton priory, the chancel at
St. Chad Stafford, St. Alban's slype, Cleeve porch and the
chapter-houses of Durham and Bristol (20), with a curious
alternative on the west wall of the latter; an excellent example
of its use upon a font is at Screveton. The arcade design was
turned into surface patterning on the walls of the chapter-
house at Much Wenlock: other all-over patterns are used on the
walls of the chapter-house at Bristol (20), Christchurch nave,
and for the decoration of the huge cylindrical piers in place of
painting in a variety of designs, diamonds, chevrons, reeds and
the twist at Durham, Dumfermline, Kirby Lonsdale, Llandis-
farne, Selby, Norwich and Waltham. All-over patterning was
also used on the exterior on the gables at Lincoln and Southwell,
Caistor tower and Christchurch turret.

FONTS have shared with doorways in their preservation from these earlier times, and there remain large numbers of every type, square, circular and odd shapes, made of stone, marble and metal. In the earliest form they are without stem, squat and generally of bowl form. The common decoration is the arcade with or without figures, or intersected as at Alphington and Porchester. Others are enriched with the liveliest grotesques, especially a group centring in and around Herefordshire, of which Castle Frome, Eardisley, Holdgate, Shobdon, Stafford St. Mary and Stottesden are examples. Lead fonts are decorated with ornate arcades having seated figures; two fine examples are at Dorchester and Walton-on-the-Hill; there are standing figures at Ashover, Wareham (189, 190) and Lower Halston. Many seem to have been cast from the same mould, such as Frampton-on-Severn (191), Oxenhall, Sandhurst and Tidenham where figures alternate with scrollwork, which has been copied in stone at Coleshill. There is a fine font at Brighton depicting the Last Supper, and a feeble copy of it at North Grinston. Stanton Fitzwarren (58) and Southrop have a series of armed knights trampling upon their foes; on the arches above are engraved the names of the virtues, while the vices are named below. An imported shop font made of black marble found at Tournai and distributed in Belgium, France, and Germany is also found in a few places in England easily accessible from the sea; four in Hampshire, two in Lincolnshire, and one in Suffolk; they are of large size, square in shape with shallow bowls supported upon a central drum with additional corner columns. They are carved with figure subjects closely related to bronze castings, and decorated with medallions of doves and grapes reminiscent of Byzantine art. The finest is in the cathedral at Winchester, possibly the gift of Henry of Blois, bishop of Winchester 1129–71.

During the last half of the twelfth century surface carving rapidly diminished, giving place to work of a new order which, although of a startling nature, was the immediate outcome of the adoption of the pointed arch for constructional purposes. This type of arch was not new, for it is found in the intersecting wall arcades of the early twelfth century, but it had not been used in connection with constructional work, in which however it proved to be the complete answer to all the puzzling and difficult problems of vaulting, which had beset and befogged the mason in his endeavours to make a success of erecting a stone vault over an unequal space; at the same time it also revolutionised building ideals.

Although the early amateur rough-and-ready walling had

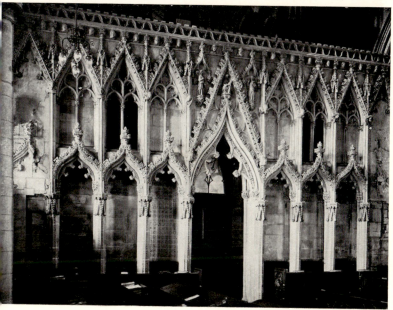

21 LICHFIELD NAVE TRIFORIUM
22 EAST SIDE SOUTHWELL PULPITUM

23 ELY CATHEDRAL, LADY CHAPEL WALL ARCADING

given place to the finished product of the master mason, there is still cause to wonder at the rapid change which took place from the earlier twelfth century methods to the amazing developments of the last years of the century and the commencement of the thirteenth. For a time the pointed arch was used sporadically; except where vaulting was required, it mingled with the round arch still in use for windows and doorways and occasionally for main arcades; however the freedom given to the mason by the use of the pointed arch quickly produced, as at Salisbury, that upward thrust which was to be the keynote of mediaeval architecture. The advent of the Cistercian Order in 1128 with its economy of materials was an important factor in this change, and no doubt influenced the absence of enrichment so noticeable in such great buildings as Salisbury and the quires of Hexham and Southwell; this dictum however does not apply to the west, where Abbey Cwm Hir, Abbey Dore, Llandaff and Worcester have their full quota of foliaged decoration, and especially in the marvellous Wells, commenced in 1189, the precursor of the mediaeval style born fully fledged during the last years of that century.

With the mastery of the main problem, buildings rose to greater heights, with an economy of materials undreamt of by the earlier masons; not however to those extravagant experiments attempted in the Ile-de-France, for we were ever a cautious people. The earlier need to cover up constructional deficiencies by surface decoration had disappeared, and the mason thought more about the proportions and mouldings of his buildings than of any necessity to decorate them. What enrichment was employed was architectural in character, but he had at this time fallen in love with the gable, which he used unsparingly; at Salisbury there are seven gables, at Worcester six and at Beverley five, these last extraordinarily attenuated and slender. The gable was used for doorways, porches, reredos, sedilia, piscina and for tomb design.

The change appears in the quire at Canterbury 1175, Oxford 1160–80, the western transepts at Ely 1174–89, the Galilee at Durham 1175 and the western chapel at Glastonbury 1185–1200. The masons who worked under the influence of the Benedictine Order were slower to assimilate the Cistercian ideals, and continued the use of the round arch and abundant decoration. The western transept at Ely is crowded both within and without with tiers of differing types of wall-arcading and surface ornament, until there is hardly a square foot of plain walling to be found (32). The windows are enriched like some important doorway with either round or pointed heads. The turrets have

D

no less than eight tiers of arcading, a veritable last fling of twelfth century profusion.

A characteristic feature of the early thirteenth century work is to be found not only in the sharpness of the gabling but also in the extraordinary heights to which the narrow lancet windows were taken; this is emphasised in the north-east, beginning with the western façades at Brinkburn and Lanercost, the north transept at Hexham and in the smaller churches at Bywell, Corbridge and Haltwhistle, continued in the north transept at York. In other districts the façades are broken up by two or three tiers of windows, as at Salisbury, Beverley, Darlington, Ely and Lincoln. Brinkburn however is a good example of the early mixing of styles, the east gable in three tiers, long lancets to the transepts and nave, and an indiscriminate use of round and pointed heads to the windows.

Apart from foliaged capitals and figure sculpture, described elsewhere (pp. 26, 32), the wall arcade still dominated the scene. It was employed upon the great fronts of Wells and Salisbury as well as on more ordinary occasions at Darlington and Lanercost. It also appeared in clerestory design, outside at York, Hereford and Darlington, and inside at Lanercost, York transepts, Hedon, Jedburgh, Chester St. John and the triforium of the cathedral there. It is however upon the ground floor that it can best be studied, as in the chapter-houses at Lincoln and Salisbury (3, 147). It is used singly in the quire at Southwell, St. Augustine Bristol, Hexham, the nine altars Durham, and as sedilia at Hedon and Haltwhistle. At Beverley it follows with charming effect the stairs to the destroyed chapter-house, and equally so to the refectory pulpit at Chester. Within the porch at Wells the mouldings are intersected, and the arcades are superimposed at Lincoln and the west porch at Ely; there is also a delightful doubled arch in the fragment of the pulpitum which once adorned the nave at Salisbury. Gables and arcades became the standard design for tombs, the former at Great Brington 1275, the latter at York on the tombs of Archbishop Grey 1255, and Sewell de Bovill 1258; it retains its round head in the lovely fragment from the shrine of St. Swithun at Winchester, and is found upon fonts, as at Ashbourne, but this period was not too successful in its church furniture, which remained heavy and a little dull.

Pointed doorways were now general, though the two transept doorways at Beverley are round-headed, flanked however by acutely pointed arches. The trefoil was often employed, as in the doorways at Corbridge and Shifnal. The one enriched moulding remaining, the dog-tooth (24), was in direct descent

26 GLOUCESTER ABBEY
FOURTEENTH CENTURY BALL-
FLOWER ORNAMENT

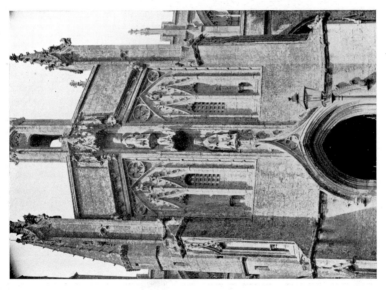

25 SOUTH PORCH, NORTHLEACH

24 DRYBURGH ABBEY
THIRTEENTH CENTURY
DOGTOOTH

TREATMENT AND DESIGN OF FOLIAGE

EARLY FOURTEENTH, NATURALISTIC   LATER FOURTEENTH, BULBOUS TREATMENT   THIRTEENTH CENTURY TREFOIL

EXETER CATHEDRAL

EXETER CATHEDRAL

CARLISLE CATHEDRAL

from the earlier nail-head; it was in constant requisition round arcade arches, as in the north transept at Hereford, over windows at Southwell, down their sides at Beverley and for ever in use to enrich doorways and porches, together with vaulting ribs. Vaulting bosses have trefoiled foliage at Southwell, figure-work in the chapter-house at Oxford and the Lady chapel at Chester, as well as the undercroft at Wells, at which place is a lovely fragment of a foliated gable-cross now placed in the cloisters.

In these earlier ages the ascetics were in combat with the world and their attitude is fully reflected in the architecture of the time, first in the early fortress-monasteries of the late eleventh and early twelfth centuries, and later in the soaring aloofness of the early thirteenth. This austerity was however not of long continuance, and as the century advanced architecture became less detached, with here and there a suggestion of the human touch. Single lancets were grouped together under an arch and through bar-tracery became homogeneous, the arched head finally filled with geometric tracery, which was copied in the wall arcading in Lincoln angel quire, Thornton abbey chapter-house, and York vestibule; in doorways at Tintern, triforiums at Lichfield, piscinas at Chester and tombs (Bp. Bridport 1264 at Salisbury and Bp. Aquablanca 1270 at Hereford (75) and in woodwork in the stalls at Winchester (87)). These architectural forms could in the later stages condescend to a happy radiance of womanly charm, as shown in the nave at Lichfield cathedral, in the proportionate design of the arcade, the attractive beauty of the triforium and the amusing treatment of geometric forms in the clerestory, comprising a human document in which harmony of purpose and design are in complete accord, and the atmosphere of springtime and fertility is in the air.

Before the close of the thirteenth century this spring had arrived, the carvers turning for a time from abstract forms, and revelling in a study of nature, carving transcriptions to a new purpose. For a quarter of a century this release from convention enabled them to produce work which was a marvellous combination of observation and technical excellence. It is found as early as 1285 in the shrine base of St. Cantelupe at Hereford, and in the shrine bases for St. Frideswide, Oxford 1289 and St. Alban 1305, and may be noted in the canopies of Bp. Louth's tomb at Ely 1298 and a wall tomb in the chapel of St. James at Exeter 1310. The same observance is the predominant note of the eastern side of the reredos at Beverley, in the arcading round the chapter-houses at York and Southwell, the lavatory

SUFFOLK TOWER PARAPETS, WOODBRIDGE AND WALBERSWICK
F. T. Baggallay, del.

a t Hexham, and the canopy round the font at Luton. Perhaps it s finest flowering is to be found at Exeter, where William de M ontacute 1310 was responsible for the carving of the bosses an d corbels of the quire and ambulatory (27).

There was also a change in the form of window tracery; ge ometrical designs had been fully exploited, and the ramifica tions of the latest patterning gave way before the oncoming o f the ogee curve, which presently permeated all decorative m otifs. The ogee was first used in what is called reticulated tracery, but quickly became free and flamelike (34), shown in the east windows at Fishlake and Welwick, both in Yorkshire.

THE SOUTH PORCH, MENDLESHAM CHURCH, SUFFOLK
F. T. Baggallay, del.

The fourteenth century masons having tried out flowing tracery, became enamoured with it, and the salient feature of their designs henceforward, whether for window, canopy, or tomb, was the ogee curve with its wavy lines flowing and intermingling the patterning becoming ever more intricate and lovely. This they did without considering the stone required for these exceptional forms, or the glass worker whose business it was to fill in these extraordinary forms with scenes and figures without unduly distorting their anatomy. The admirable skill with which the sculptor accomplished this problem can be seen in the canopy of the Percy tomb at Beverley 1340 (6, 169) where the Annunciation, Coronation, and many other subjects are ingeniously designed to fill the queerest shapes with which craftsmen were ever asked to deal. The York school was an adept in this particular class of work, shown at Welwick, Bainton, Cartmel and Hull, the details of which we must leave for further consideration.

The gable with simple or foiled arches is used in the pulpitum at Southwell, the feretory at Selby, the Easter sepulchre at Lincoln, the Rood screen at St. Albans, and Patrington and Heckington fonts, and there are noble examples in the canopies over the tombs of Aveline, Valence and Crouchback in Westminster abbey. The ball-flower moulding (26) succeeded the dog-tooth in favour but was not produced so freely. It is found however in profusion round the windows at Gloucester, Leominster and Ledbury, on the tomb canopies at Bristol and on prior Sutton's tomb at Oxford 1320 (76).

The second quarter of the fourteenth century showed the return to the architectural treatment of foliage, this time almost square in shape, bulged out in the centre and rippled round the edges; this lasted in a modified form until the end of the mediaeval period. It was an ideal shape for the now fashionable cusping and finialled ogee gables, which were the predominating note of this time. It is the principal feature of the sedilias at Dorchester, Ripon, Southwell, Nantwich and Patrington, also the glorious set at Exeter; in the arcading round the feretory at Winchester, Beverley nave, and the magnificent arcading round the Lady chapel at Ely 1321-49 (23) which was enriched with sculpture recording incidents in the life of the Virgin, the diaper work was originally covered with gold and brilliant in colour. It appears in the piscinas at Exeter and Chester, the Easter sepulchre at Hawton and Heckington, the screens of Boughton and Gt. Bardfield and the shrines at Stanton Harcourt and Lincoln. The fonts of this period are of much interest, such as those at Burford, Fishlake, Hedon, Hitchin, Hull, Howden, Northampton and Rattlesden; there is a tendency in some examples for the stem shape to disappear, the straight line of the head being carried down to the step. Diapering of the walls is found in abundance at Southwell and Lincoln, in the screenwork, pulpitums and canopy work above the quire at Wells. The exterior parapets are pierced with trefoils, as at Tewkesbury, or ogees as at Malmesbury and Heckington.

If the first 150 years had been influenced through the regular Orders, the middle period may be considered as both secular and civic, just as the final phase was parochial. This mid-period was colourful with pageantry and bright with chivalry, for knights and their ladies, together with their arms, share the honours with the saints and their emblems, with whom they

30 LAUNCESTON SOUTH AISLE
31 BARFREYSTONE DOORHEAD

TWELFTH AND FIFTEENTH CENTURY APPLIED WALL DECORATION, ARCADING AND PANELLING were associated in canopied decoration. The great cathedrals and monasteries were often governed by politically minded bishops who held important offices under the crown, travelling in state with large retinues and spreading their magnificence before the people; nevertheless they spent freely in enlarging and beautifying the churches which contained their thrones, furnishing them with munificence and taste. It is only necessary to recall the works done by the succeeding bishops of Exeter, Lincoln and York, and in the monastic cathedrals of Ely and Winchester, to realise how much these buildings owe to their energy and care. The fourteenth century indeed produced a magnificent harvest of supreme craftsmanship which unfortunately for us was largely destroyed at the suppression.

This pageantry was however cut short in the middle of the century by the Black Death, whose repeated ravages gradually decimated the population and reduced the country to prostration. When work was resumed it was with a different outlook, sobered by the nearness of death, which forever after was rarely absent from the thoughts of the people, and contributed largely to the new-found affection for their parish churches and the establishment of chantries and gilds.

The dominant feature of the thirteenth century architecture had been the soaring vertical lines of shaft, window and gable; in the following century these features were broadened out as well as enriched, the bowing ogee arches closely cusped, the spandrels filled with admirable figure and foliage carving. For the last two hundred years however, excepting for certain of the earlier pinnacled tombs and spired stallwork, the trend was ever toward the horizontal line, which became more and more accentuated in tomb and stallwork design to the close of the fifteenth century. In the south, during the early years of the sixteenth century, English tradition was weakened by the introduction of foreign craftsmen who at the invitation of the Court practised an alien style having no affinity to native thought, and whose influence proved the undoing of an unbroken continuity of work lasting over three hundred years. The native architecture of the fifteenth century owed but little if indeed anything to continental procedure; it was insular in construction and English in thought and practice. Our nineteenth century restorers have christened this horizontal style "Perpendicular"; and curiously enough spoken of it in a deprecating and condescending manner; nevertheless it was the individualistic treatment of mediaeval architecture in our island, self-sufficient, sensible and restrained, the means fashioned to the end in view, as the reduction of the wall veil to a minimum for the admission of windows filled with coloured glass. The roofs both of stone and timber are not to be surpassed, and differ in design from anything to be found over the water; where, we may ask, are there other vaults in Europe to compete with such examples as are to be found at St. Frideswide's Oxford (7) or the Divinity School in the same city; those at Sherborne, Henry VII's chapel at Westminster and the fan vaults at Bath abbey and King's college chapel at Cambridge? If we turn to timber, the single and double hammer-beam roofs of East Anglia (153, 154) and the lovely panelled beam roofs in other parts of the country are unique. The splendid series of towers in Somerset and the churches erected by the munificence of the wool merchants, to name a few of the many, are all work which is splendid in conception and thoroughly English in character.

The horizontal line and closely ranged nichework are the principal keynotes of fifteenth century design. These are to be found in the majority of porches, which if they have not actually a flat crown are but slightly cambered; the aisles are no longer gabled and the battlemented parapets have the same effect as the string courses inside the building, breaking the upright lines of roof support. It is however in the furnishing and enrichment of the building that this lack of upward thrust becomes insistent. The serried tiered rows of niched figures on the west fronts at Exeter (68) and Beverley are matched within by the great screens placed behind the high altars at Winchester, St. Albans, Southwark, Christchurch, Milton Abbas and at All Souls college chapel at Oxford, completed as many of them are by a deep horizontal cresting (36). This horizontality is continued in sedilia at Gloucester, Furness, St. Davids, Adderbury, Maids Moreton and elsewhere, and in reredos design at Ludlow, Wells Lady chapel, and the transeptal chapels at St. Cuthbert's in the same city; also at Somerton, and in the chantry chapel reredoses at St. Albans, Gloucester, Wells, Winchester, and Worcester. The horizontal line is prominent in tomb design especially in the fabrics of chantry chapels at St. Albans, Boxgrove, Exeter, Gloucester, Tewkesbury, Wells and Winchester (80) and in tomb canopies at Exeter, Ewelme, Bristol St. Mark, Gt. Brington, and at Acton, Cheshire, Wingfield, Woodleigh, Wells, Long Ashton, to name only a few.

Nichework, pinnacles and blind tracery or panelling are the chief sources of design in this period, be it in stone or wood; they form the decorative features of the work mentioned above. The pinnacle motif could be taken to extraordinary lengths, as in the chantry chapels of Waynfleete and Beaufort at Winchester

35 ELY CATHEDRAL, BISHOP ALCOCK'S CHANTRY

34 ST. MARY, BEVERLEY, FLEMISH CHAPEL

AN EXAMPLE OF FIFTEENTH CENTURY ELABORATION IN NICHEWORK

36 WINCHESTER CATHEDRAL, TOP OF THE GREAT ALTAR SCREEN

(80), the reredos at Durham and the canopy over the tomb of Lord Spencer 1370 at Tewkesbury (alas, almost entirely renewed). It is found in the reredos of Prince Arthur's chantry at Worcester, and in the pulpitums at Canterbury (5) and York, which are in fact a copy of woodcraft made by the mason. Canopies over niches, although no longer spiring, were a complicated mass of ogee archlets, pinnacles and miniature vaultings, excellently shown in both the Alcock and West chantries at Ely (4, 35), and in single niches at Beverley St. Mary, and Mold, as well as the simplified version over the pulpit at Arundel. These units of design are employed in the decoration of the fonts at Ewelme, Laxfield, Redgrave and Walsoken (59) and the pulpits at Swymbridge, North Cerney and Northleach. Tracery is used on the Stanton Harcourt font, Nantwich pulpit, Ramrynge's and Fox's chantry chapels at St. Albans and Winchester respectively, and the use of surface decoration on the front of the porch and gildhall at Cirencester (33), the north porch at Beverley Minster, as well as the interior walls of the quire at Gloucester.

Surface decoration is fairly plentiful both for inside and exterior walls. In the flint districts rich designs were made by a combination of Caen stone and flints (pp. 20, 21) as at Gt. Barton, Earl Stonham clerestory, Eye, Worlingworth and Walsham-le-Willows porches, and at Southwold and many other East Anglia churches. In Cornwall at Launceston the exterior of the church is entirely covered with surface carving (30), and at Devizes (2) and Bromham magnificent results are obtained by elaborately enriched battlements with pinnacles and towering niches, for both of which the same mason was undoubtedly responsible.

E

THE EVOLUTION IN THE DECORATION OF THE PIER-CAPITAL

THE evolution in the shape of the pier-cap and its decoration is an epitome in miniature of the development of foliage and flower design in stone cutting, from its tardy beginnings in the eleventh century to its full flowering in the thirteenth and fourteenth, and to its final decline by the close of the fifteenth, although in the south-west there was a revival of pier-cap decoration in the early sixteenth century. In this study we must concentrate our attention on what took place in England, with but a passing glance at the possible origins in both form and style found elsewhere. In Normandy the cap had a traceable but embryonic affinity to the Roman capital, confined however to the volute, which supported the corners of the abacus, and which eventually grew into the *crochet* capital of the Ile-de-France. After the Conquest this type of cap is but rarely found in England, though early examples of it are at Lastingham 1078–88, in the chapel of Durham castle, and Blyth priory founded 1088, which however was an alien house attached to St. Katherine of Rouen.

Its place was taken by the cushion capital, a survival from the Anglo-Saxon period, whose origin may be traced through Germany to Byzantium, and which was unknown in Normandy until introduced later from England. This capital reverted to first principles; it was an impost block, square above, circular beneath where it crowned the column; above this was placed a second block from which sprang the arches, preventing their weight from splitting away the edges of the capping. The sides of the cushion were cut spherically, the points meeting at the corners, the surface beneath rounded away, the abacus above chamfered back on its lower edge. This plain surface soon attracted decoration of a rudimentary kind, of which there are several varieties, including all-over patterning composed of basket-work, such as may be seen in remote civilisations even today, and is figured in a cap in Selby nave triforium (37), and also in the churches of Campsall Yorks, and Ducklington Oxon. This type developed into Celtic patterning, as in the cloister doorways at Ely, the western portal at St. Bees, Rochester, York crypt and a fine series of caps at St. Albans, now divorced from their original setting in the slype. Further examples with figures and grotesques are at Adel, Brayton,

37 SELBY ABBEY TRIFORIUM
39 SELBY ABBEY TRIFORIUM
41 WELLS CATHEDRAL NAVE

38 MALMESBURY NAVE
40 SHREWSBURY ST. MARY NAVE
42 LICHFIELD CATHEDRAL NAVE

43 BRIDLINGTON PRIORY NORTH PORCH
44 SOUTHWELL CHAPTER-HOUSE
45 DEVON, WOLBOROUGH NAVE
46 BLOXHAM CHURCH, OXON
47 ALNWICK CHURCH, NORTHUMBERLAND

Kilpeck, Leonard Stanley and Romsey, and in loose caps found at Hereford, Winchester and York.

The main stream of design was flowing however in a different direction; the cushion capital, in place of having a large single semicircle upon each face, was divided into a number of smaller half-circles placed round the top of the impost, projecting downwards to the necking and forming a series of cones, each cone separated from its neighbour by a baguette or arrow-headed fluting called a reed. This became further elaborated, and many varieties were used around the drums of the great cylindrical piers (38) and upon the squared and grouped shafted capitals as well as in the wall arcades. Although the cone continued, it was marked later by another change in form, the convex shape of the impost becoming concave, suggesting a vegetable growth, although at first the cones were still enriched by borderings; this type sprang up in the west of England and formed a link between the Norman and the bell-shaped Corinthianesque; as it developed it resembled a pollarded willow tree, the cones uncurving and cut off short and sharp, becoming hollow trumpets from which suggestions of leafage sprouted, budding later into blossoms of wondrous fertility. The remarkable invention of the following years deserves a volume to itself, every imaginable idea seems to have been tried out; the pier-caps from the arcades at St. Mary at Shrewsbury (40) contain sufficient material to last a modern designer for a lifetime. It was a period in which the artist within the man stood tip-toe on the threshold of a new world of possibilities; he was tired of the imponderable heaviness of abstract Norman art and longed for the freedom which now seemed within his grasp. Carving with a fresh impetus and a renewed impatience, he produced a storehouse of experiments in the shortest imaginable time, that today leave us wondering why, with so much to use, he should have been content to fall back upon the conventionalised lily trefoil (41), which can be as tiresome as it can be lovely, and which certainly outlasted its welcome by constant repetition; here again the south-west produced its own version in a windswept form, blown round pier-cap and bestrewn upon corbel with the greatest charm and felicitious grace.

Two side streams added their quota to the general total of early pier-cap design in England, first in the rebuilding of Canterbury cathedral, by the introduction of the *crochet* capital from the Ile-de-France which was also used in the reconstruction of the retroquire at Chichester; this type was also used at Oakham castle and Lincoln cathedral, and in the retention of the volute at St. Frideswide's Oxford, Gt. Bedwyn, Ducklington, Frodsham, Tilney All Saints and in the experiments at Shrewsbury. The fragments from the destroyed cloisters at Bridlington and Southwark also show unmistakable evidence of their classic or Byzantine origins through French channels. These early cloisters of convents were store houses of symbolic carvings and embody the tortuous and twisted myths of the time embedded in rich Celtic convolutions; they were a place for meditation, and the carver seized his opportunity to place his work before the contemplative mind. Cloisters at this time were neither vaulted nor enclosed, the earliest vaulted and windowed cloister being that at Westminster, begun 1245. Before that date they had a wooden pentice roof which was held in position on the garth side by a colonnade of small arches supported upon twin columns, a design not only charming in itself but serving the purpose of strengthening the colonnade against the thrust of the roof. No complete example of this early type has come down to us in England, but fragments have been found and small sections have been re-erected at Westminster, Bridlington, Kirkstall and Newminster, and there are more fragments at Norwich, Southwark and Winchester. It was the elaboration of the cloister carvings which caused St. Bernard to strike out at the extravagance of the times in his writings, in which he says:—

"Again in the cloisters, what is the meaning of these ridiculous monsters, of that deformed beauty, that beautiful deformity, before the very eyes of the brethren when reading? What are disgusting monkeys there for, or ferocious lions, or monstrous centaurs, or spotted tigers, or fighting soldiers, or huntsmen sounding the bugle? . . . Such endless forms appear everywhere, that it is more pleasant to read in the stonework than in books, and to spend the day admiring these oddities than in meditating on the law of God."

The arrival in England of the Cistercian Order, bringing with them their Burgundian type of architecture, was the second stream which altered the whole trend of building design for a generation. Missionaries of austerity and plainness, they opposed the luxurious architectural character of the Cluniacs and Benedictines, and for a generation they practised what they preached, with the result of an architecture refined and full of quality, relying entirely upon proportions and mouldings for its effect. One form of decoration which seems to have been in use even in their earlier buildings was the plantin or water-leaf, this appears sparingly upon pier-cap and corbel. Its striking note is that the leaves were curled upwards and inwards whereas the *crochet* volute was turned outwards and downwards. Its use is particularly noticeable in the north and west, and is admirably shown at Buildwas, Byland, Fountains, Furness, Cultram, Newminster and Roche. Later it appears in the Benedictine and Augustinian architecture, and in the parochial churches which came under their influence and adapted their building methods as at Selby, Beverley, and Ripon, Shrewsbury St. Mary; and at Brandsburton, St. Michael Spurriergate in York, North Leigh and Little Faringdon in Oxon.

Reverting to the main decorative movement of pier-cap design, we find as already noted that the promise of the transitional period was abandoned for an architectural foliage, which after all was a poor substitute for the variety already exhibited; this trefoil foliage was in direct descent from the Byzantine acanthus, with the elements of the Corinthian capital transformed and used to a new purpose by the alembic of the carver's mind, and it quickly assumed complete sway. Considering the smallness of the unit employed, the results are wonderful, the treatment varying from extreme simplicity to abounding luxuriance, both growth and treatment varied to meet the requirements of the moment. In the south transept at Wells are carved the last of the cones and cornucopias from which the foliage sprang; when the carvers had reached the nave, the stalks grew straight from the necking of the bell-cap and turned over with a wealth of knop-like foliage (41). The leaves vary, some are trefoils, others quatrefoils or cinquefoils; at St. Frideswide's Oxford they remain stiff and erect, at Gt. Bedwyn although on a square capital the knops are all nodding towards the left as if blown by the wind. At Shrewsbury the stalks, mutually crossing each other, are split and threaded through one another. The work of the west is vigorous, as in the windswept foliage at Abbey Dore, Llandaff, Llanidloes (from Abbey-cwm-Hir), Shrewsbury, Wells and Worcester. At West Walton the foliage grows wreathwise, the undercutting extraordinarily clever. In the north porch at Bridlington (43) the foliage forms lilies bursting into lovely blossoms, the perfect type of conventional blooming. In the west porch at Ely the thirteenth century carvers vied with the twelfth in overloading capitals and mouldings with scintillating ornament—the shafts are crocketted, the foliage of the capitals hanging down by their own weight, whilst the chevron moulding is transfigured into small trefoiled leaves and flowers.

Towards the close of this period there came a loosening of architectural restraint in the forms displayed by the carvers; indeed they seem to have been carried away by their own cleverness. In the nave at Lichfield (42) the foliage of the capitals is as luxuriant as the undergrowth of a hedgerow in May when subjected to wind and rain; it is less stately and more tumbled than before, but is a marvellous technical achievement with superb undercutting. In the Lady chapel at Chester a vaulting corbel suggests the oncoming of naturalism in foliage treatment—the leaves are no longer trefoils, and it indicates the movement which with rapidity was to find its climax in the glories of the chapter-house at Southwell.

For the first quarter or even less of the fourteenth century the carvers became the delineators of the nature they saw around them, producing with great delicacy a close study of it; what they gained however in grace they lost in architectural significance. The foliage of the capital no longer springs from the necking, following its hollow bell-shape, but gradually becomes wreathed round the hollow, almost hiding its form. This short spring of loveliness may best be studied in the chapter-house at Southwell (44), the quire at Exeter, the reredos at Beverley and in Selby quire, York chapter-house, Wells ambulatory, Lichfield quire, Beverley wall arcades, St. Frideswide's Oxford and in such a church as Claypole, Notts. At Southwell the stalks still spring from a horizontal line above the necking, the carving however is no longer architectural but an added enrichment, profuse and almost staggering in its technical mastery of mind over matter, in so far that in many of the capitals the leafage seems to have been pinned on and is not homogeneous with its setting. In the quire at Exeter upon the vaulting corbels (27) and the ambulatory bosses (141) there is a mine of English woodland plant-form in which squirrels, caterpillars and other animals and creeping things disport themselves. The same may be said of the bosses of the vaulting behind the reredos at Beverley and the shrine base of St. Frideswide at Oxford, together with the bosses in the Lady chapel vault there. At Beverley, Claypole, Lichfield, Selby, Wells, and York the foliage is wreathed round the capitals without any pretence of growth and becomes redundant decoration added to an already finely moulded pier-cap.

It is from this point that the decoration of pier-cap and corbel gradually disappears. The moulded capital was from the start often in the same building as the foliaged pier-cap, and they had as it were appeared side by side, the second predominating, but from this point onwards the reverse becomes noticeable, until by the fifteenth century the moulded capital is the rule, the enriched pier-cap the exception. Until the Black Death however, decoration was continued, as in the quire at Carlisle, the nave corbels at Exeter, the wall arcades of the nave at

48 MALMESBURY PORCH LUNETTE
49 GLASTONBURY NORTH DOORWAY

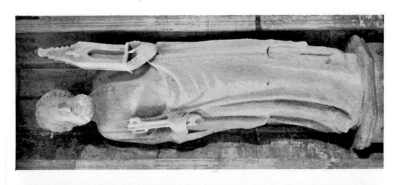

LATE TWELFTH CENTURY FIGURES ORIGINALLY DECORATING A PORTAL TO CHAPTER-HOUSE
FOURTEENTH CENTURY FIGURES FROM VARIOUS PARTS OF HOWDEN CHURCH NOW COLLECTED

Beverley and in such a church as Patrington, but to realise the new form of foliage design we must turn to examine the canopy of the Percy tomb at Beverley and the sedilia at Exeter. The new mode was an architectural setting of naturalistic foliage known as bulbous, from the tendency of each leaf to be humped in the centre and rippled round the edges and the leaf becoming almost square in shape. To the close of the whole period it never lost these characteristics, although the leaves became more squared in shape but less protruberant in modelling. During the fourteenth century other forms of decoration in addition to foliage were in use, such as paterae (small squares of ornament spaced round the bell), and in Oxfordshire a group of churches have their capitals decorated with demi-figures of men and women; Adderbury, Bloxham (46), Hampton Powle, Hanwell and Woodstock, also at Ludgershall; however in many examples extra mouldings were employed and the spacing for decoration thereby diminished.

In the fifteenth century it is rare to find a decorated capital, though in the south-west, especially in Devon, there are many arcades with foliated and decorated capitals, as at Bishopsteinton, Bradnich, Pinhoe, Stokenham, Swymbridge, Tor Brian, Whimple, Wolborough (45), with many other places. In this particular type mouldings seem to play a small part, and at Bishopsteinton they almost disappear; amongst the foliage appear heads, beasts and birds in addition to twisted scrolls and ribbon-work, the latter combined at Ottery St. Mary with elephants' heads; ribbon-work may also be noticed on the pier-caps of Little Malvern priory in Worcestershire. Another type of decoration is the use of demi-angels holding shields reminiscent of tomb format; these are placed at the four cardinal points and may be seen at Alphington, Rewe, Stoke-in-Teignhead, and also at Pilton in Somerset. If however we desire to see what the fifteenth century craftsmen could execute in foliage design we must turn to the woodmen, whose lovely trails of vine, oak, hawthorn, rose and pomegranate enrich their screens, as the foliated bosses decorate their panelled timber roofs.

THE WORK OF THE SCULPTOR

"The art of the past remains with us, when the fruits of other noble endeavours have crumbled away. Through this we experience the sensations of many admirable lives, and through it we share in a sensation of success which probably may never be ours. Art is the evidence of man's opposition to mere necessity and chance, and the nearest approximation to a sense of immortality."

Self Portrait, CHARLES RICKETTS

IT is a major disaster that figure sculpture, the finest and most representative work of the mediaeval craftsmen, should be the one to suffer demolition and damage, not entirely from neglect and the weather, but principally from the greed and malice of men. Exterior statues, especially those which were placed at almost inaccessible heights, have often escaped deliberate destruction when the interior figurework, other than on memorials, has been destroyed. Certain sculpture carved in freestones, marble and alabaster, though worn and broken, is still worthy of study, but figurework in other materials is difficult to come by. Bronze effigies to the number of ten have been spared of the many of which descriptions survive; those in precious metals we only know about from hearsay—they were raped, stolen, and melted down for the value of the material, a known example the silver plates with which the wooden statue of Henry V was adorned at Westminster.

The sculpture of mediaeval times differed from that of the Greeks and Romans which went before and the Renaissance which came after, in that it was anonymous. In the thirteenth and fourteenth centuries it was masonic in origin, and there would appear to have been numbers of masons who were qualified to build, carve, or produce excellent sculpture and be equally proficient in them all. In the building accounts of Westminster Abbey it is rare to find the entry of a craftsman as a professional sculptor. Again unlike Greek work, which we have come to regard as our criterion of sculpture, the majority of mediaeval figurework was carved in coarse freestones, and was homogeneous with the architecture it adorned, making no pretensions to be an individual figure set up by itself to be seen and admired in the round. Architectural sculpture was never unduly finished, especially for exterior positions, and the higher it was placed the more sketchy it became, a study of masses with strong light and shade, where a delicate finish would have

54   WELLS CATHEDRAL, CONTINUATION OF THE GREAT WESTERN ICONOSTASIS ROUND THE
NORTH-WESTERN TOWER

FIGURE DETAIL, EARLY AND LATE, FROM THIRTEENTH TO FIFTEENTH CENTURIES

resulted in smoothing away the strength and beauty of the whole conception.

If we study records and examine churches it is at once apparent that from the thirteenth century onwards figure sculpture was the crowning feature of all churches both inside and out, designed in all sizes from the noble figures on the west front of the cathedral at Wells (54) to the miniature weepers round the tombs at Westminster Abbey. Reredoses such as those at Winchester, St. Albans, Southwark had no doubt their ranges of freestone figures coloured and gilt; as at Durham, Christchurch and Exeter they were of gilded alabaster, or of wood plated with silver and studded with jewels.

Figure sculpture strongly reflects the architecture of the time in which it was produced. The work of the twelfth century is immature, heavy, coarse and uninspired; that of the thirteenth century, on the contrary, is full of inspiration, graceful, aloof and attenuated, showing a complete control of the medium employed. The fourteenth century was richly decorative, humane and spectacular, using elaboration for its own sake, whereas the fifteenth century, especially after the Black Death, is both sober and restrained, with a quiet dignity, lacking however in personal feeling. It was during the latter part of the mediaeval period that the production of figurework came under the control of gilds and shop tradition, in which the mason had but little part to play. Carving of importance was no longer carried out in the masons' yards closely connected with the erection of a particular building, but was executed and sent from centres such as London, Bristol, York and Chelleston, losing in architectural significance more than it gained in slickness of technique.

In the seventh century in and around Northumbria there was a period during which sculpture of the finest quality was produced; the Ruthwell and Bewcastle crosses still stand to prove this fact along with other work of less magnitude. There is the torso of the Virgin at York and the panels now at Chichester of later date than the crosses; the art of the Saxon times was inspired, but from what particular quarter is best left to the antiquaries. The Winchester illuminations, the carving of ivories, and the efforts of the Irish craftsmen, justify the assertion that in spite of wars and conquests the arts of Britain not only continued but at times flourished. Between the Northumbrian crosses and the Norman Conquest two other sources influenced early design, that of the Vikings of inferior quality, and the later Saxon work in Wessex; however, William brought this interesting art to a sudden end, destroying much of it, and for the remainder of the century figurework ceased to exist;

F

when it reappeared in the twelfth century it was primitive and crude, with no pretensions to either good design or workmanship. These Norman carvings are to be found upon fonts and the tympanums of doorways, derived from the earlier Norse influence with its beak-heads, Anglo-Saxon tradition, and the gradual percolation of fresh ideas from the south of France. Another source came from the study of the works of the goldsmiths, the metalworkers and the carvers of ivories, which were the possessions of the convents; from these the masons could draw their inspiration as well as copy their technique. Not only did they adapt them to stonework but in casting lead fonts; after 1150 we find an altogether superior type of figure seated beneath arcading; they produced also an excellent series of matrices of seals, as the one belonging to Lincoln 1100.

The sculpture of large figures in the round was of slower growth and only became possible with the decline of the earlier type of symbolism, such as is found cut on the pier-caps dug up on the site of Reading Abbey and the capitals of the Canterbury crypt. This decline made for simplicity and a larger handling of the subject, which was no longer clogged with extraneous details. When reviewing this period we must remember that the same process was taking place throughout Western Europe, and was not confined to any particular district or country, although it often appeared individually.

A remarkable group of carvings of this time is portrayed in the south porch at Malmesbury, where in addition to the ever popular medallions, there are lunettes (48) within the porch containing almost life-sized seated figures of the Apostles, all in constrained and stiff-necked attitudes, clothed with garments reminiscent of the art of the illuminator, but in advance of other work at the time. However, at Glastonbury a few years later the figures are free from the earlier conventions, and become almost of thirteenth-century quality (49). Other doorheads are the south porch at Fishlake and Barfreston (31), where medallions are used, and the prior's doorway at Ely, where although of good quality the sculptor fails in his laboured attempt at the figures in the typanum. Other interesting sculptures are the virtues cut on the fonts at Southrop and Stanton Fitzwarren (58). Cluniac influence dominates the carving of the lavatory basin at Much Wenlock and the font at Brighton, adjacent to the important abbey of Lewes. The south-east lagged behind, and when figurework appears was influenced from the continent, as shown in the fine west portal at Rochester, which is unlike any other work we possess.

The earlier traditions of good work seem to have lingered

59 WALSOKEN, NORFOLK, FIFTEENTH CENTURY

58 STANTON FITZWARREN, TWELFTH CENTURY

SMALL FIGUREWORK DECORATING TOMBS, CHANTRIES AND WALLS, LATE FOURTEENTH AND FIFTEENTH CENTURY

62 DIVINITY SCHOOL, OXFORD

61 EXETER CATHEDRAL

60 CARTMEL PRIORY

in the north, and at Lincoln and York are the fragments of panels of differing dates and styles well in advance of their time. Lincoln has a fine west portal now unfortunately ruined by restoration. At York in the grounds of St. Mary's abbey there has been excavated the remnants of a fine doorway, probably part of the chapter-house. This includes voussoirs with seated niched figures, as well as several statues rather larger than life-size which stood on either side the portal, including St. John (50), two Apostles and Moses (51), together with a fragment of a seated Madonna; they are the earliest examples of large figures which we have, and may be dated about 1200; they are the direct antecedents of the lovely work of the thirteenth century. At Durham, panels are preserved in the library illustrating Christ's appearance after the Resurrection which for delicacy of style and technique leave little to be desired.

It is impossible in a short section to do justice to the many-sided activities of the mediaeval sculptor, even that of a single century; there are however exceptional examples of the thirteenth century which are of great importance, especially the wonderful sculptured façade or iconostasis in front of the cathedral at Wells (54). This was executed during the first half of the century, and there are still 127 out of the original 180 figures and sculpture which covered the great screen. This truly magnificent conception was carried out in great completeness, and comprises a history of the Bible and the church both on earth and in heaven. The front is peopled by saints, kings and their consorts, ecclesiastics both male and female, apostles, angels and subjects from the old and the new law (70). It looked down upon God's acre and was before the priest and people during the last offices, showing them a band of figures rising from their graves surmounted by the nine orders of angels. Nowhere else in England is to be found a scheme so complete or one so finely carried out. The whole of the work is carved from Doulting stone, of which the cathedral itself was constructed, and this mass of carving, with the exception of the central gable which is a little later, was the labour of not more than a dozen sculptors. The work shows increasingly accomplished technique as it proceeded from the earlier stiff memorial figures to the tall and graceful sculptured effigies with gentle expressions and inclined heads, their garments rippled in a manner peculiar to Wells. The façade is complete in itself, and we look in vain for a continuation of the work of the same carvers elsewhere. This front was originally painted, to which it owes its preservation. Traces of red and other colours can be faintly made out on garment and background. It was started before 1220, and Bp. Joscelin described the front as completed about a month before he died in 1242.

The transepts of Westminster abbey and the retroquire at Lincoln are also centres of lovely and delicate sculpture, placed in the triforiums and fortunately but little injured. The work consists of angels in the spandrels of window and arch, censing at Westminster, playing music at Lincoln. In them we find the highest and most perfect exposition of mediaeval thought in sculpture, dignified, gentle and remote. The superb excellence of the modelling, the poise of the figures at Westminster (66), especially on the eastern sides of the north and south transepts, with their rhythmical swing of censers, the nobility of countenance together with mastery of technique, are only matched by the angels of the Expulsion and Resurrection in the retroquire at Lincoln. This work may be placed about the middle of the century, the Westminster angels a little earlier, the Lincoln angels between the earlier type and the graver and more serenely composed angels already mentioned. Other work at both churches includes the entrance to the chapter-house at Westminster and the Judgment porch at Lincoln, of which Lethaby states that the figures "are nowhere surpassed in effective action and elevated expression and may stand with any architectural sculpture in the world." The Lincoln porch has been over-restored, the head of Christ is new, the angels should carry emblems of the Passion; nevertheless it is our finest example of a tympanum representing Christ in Judgment. On either side the doorway are the headless statues of the Church and the Synagogue, boldly cut both in pose and drapery and in the finest tradition. In the outer arch mould are a series of vesicas in the elaborate foliage (56) and in the inner moulding niches; within both are graceful, delicate miniature figures matching in technique the rest of the work. The great façade at Salisbury cannot be considered here, for it has lost almost all its mediaeval sculpture.

Of the lesser sculpture, in the spandrels of arcading, on the corbels, heads and figure subjects on capitals there is little lack of material for study; unfortunately much of it is fearfully and wonderfully restored. Wall arcading was continued from the twelfth century, and there are examples in the elder Lady chapel at Bristol 1200, Worcester east end 1210–20, Westminster transept 1250, and Salisbury chapter-house 1270 (3, 147), in addition to the choir of angels on the fragments of the pulpitum 1260. Bristol continued the earlier tradition of grotesques, such as the goat playing the fiddle. The Worcester set has a few centaurs, but the Last Judgment with its punishments, martyr-

65 WINCHESTER CATHEDRAL
THE ALMIGHTY

64 COVENTRY, ST. MARY HALL
ST. GEORGE AND DRAGON

63 WINCHESTER CATHEDRAL
MADONNA AND CHILD

1 AND 3, FRAGMENTS FROM THE REREDOS, ETC. 2 WOODEN COPY OF ALABASTER WORK

66 WESTMINSTER ABBEY, ANGEL FROM TRANSEPT TRIFORIUM

67 WARWICK, BEAUCHAMP CHAPEL, EAST WALL 1450

68 EXETER CATHEDRAL, PORTION OF WESTERN SCREEN

doms and Scriptural subjects is the principal theme, in which more than one set of carvers and times are indicated. In the chapter-house at Salisbury are marvellous pictorial scenes from the Old and New Testament which have been restored by Burges, perhaps too cleverly for our discrimination, but the charming angels with their musical instruments on the old pulpitum are untouched. Other carvings are on the vaulting bosses in the chapter-house at Oxford, the undercroft at Wells and a loose boss at Abbey Dore. Small figures on corbel supports at Oxford 1225, Durham and Wells 1260 are vigorously cut, if a few lack the technical ability to lift them from the grotesque to the living figure. In the transepts at Wells, little groups of figures are carved amongst the foliage of the pier-caps; the wayfarer, fruit stealers, or the faces of men with the toothache, all of them lively representations and extremely virile. The human figure is carved upon two stone lecterns now at Norton and Crowle, and there are innumerable heads to be found everywhere, of which those of a king, queen and bishop in the north porch at Bridlington are excellent examples (43).

With the turn of the century the natural foliage which lasted for about twenty years was interspersed with figure sculpture, shown on the quire corbels at Exeter, including a Madonna with censing angels, St. Katherine who is standing upon a corbel head of William of Montacute the carver, a tumbler and musician, and Biblical subjects. There is however no great iconostasis left during this period as at Wells; for the west front at Lichfield was thoroughly destroyed during the Civil Wars and as thoroughly restored in the nineteenth century, and is now a modern work. At Howden is a collection of rather decayed sculpture taken from the exterior of the building and now housed within the church (52, 53), but it is in the lesser carvings that we may form a judgment of the quality of the fourteenth century work.

The northern carvings have a robustness and brilliance which is difficult to match elsewhere, in tomb design especially, as in the luxuriant figurework displayed in the spandrels of the canopy of the Percy tomb at Beverley (6), where saints, knights and ladies (169, 170) mingle together beneath the figure of the Father holding the soul of Lady Percy, surrounded by adoring angels; within are charming heads and figures, and in the roof the bosses show choirs of angels playing music and singing. The Harrington tomb at Cartmel, although carved in coarse stone and lacking in finished technique, nevertheless is full of invention; the tiny figures on the standards of the Madonna and St. Katherine are lissom in pose and line (60). The subject corbels at York, Beverley, and Chester and the carved heads from the same places show a wide range of observation, thought and accomplishment. The characteristic touches of ordinary humanity depicted in the Madonna in the chapter-house at York and on a patera on the east side of the reredos at Beverley are especially noticeable, as are the heads of a queen at Beverley and a lady in a wimple at Patrington. The vaulting bosses in the reredos at Beverley including a Coronation scene (72), and at St. Mary's of angels conveying the soul to heaven, and the Annunciation on a pendant at Patrington are full of invention. The same may be said of the Easter sepulchres at Lincoln, Hawton, Patrington, Sibthorpe and Navenby. Finally the sculpture still surviving at Howden which includes figures of SS. Peter, Paul and John (52, 53); the Annunciation, bishops and a figure of the Synagogue, although weathered and broken, nevertheless gives some idea of the sway and poise in the treatment of the mass of figurework now destroyed.

In the eastern counties the main centres seem to have been at Lincoln and Peterborough: the figurework in Ancaster stone remaining is however to be found principally upon or from the towers and porches, as the statue now in the church of Terrington St. Clement. In the lesser figurework are the remains of the sculpture in clunch in the Lady chapel at Ely (23), and the lantern corbels illustrating the life of St. Etheldreda, also the charming kneeling figurines now in the West chantry. In the Midlands are the capitals with heads at Bloxham (46), Adderbury and Hanwell, as well as the Jesse window at Dorchester and the small Passion groups carved in the tracery of the east window; the tomb recesses and the Annunciation panels at Ducklington and the reredos of the Last Supper at Somerton.

Perhaps the finest work of the time of which we know the dates and particulars are the Eleanor crosses at Hardington and Geddington, Northants, and Waltham, retaining some of the splendid sculpture of 1290, most of it known to be London work. The chapter-house at Rochester illustrates the richness of the time, together with the lively figures on the cloister doorway at Norwich. Other carvings include the rescued figure of the Madonna at Winchester (63), the later work in the nave corbels and minstrels gallery at Exeter, that now taken down from the steeple of St. Mary Redcliffe and the figurework at Hereford and in the quire at Edington. There are heads at Wells, St. Albans, Glastonbury and Lichfield, bosses at Chester St. John, Exeter (74) and Worcester, and the niched figures round the fonts at Burford, Fishlake, Shilton and Tysoe. The last

69 RIPON CATHEDRAL QUIRE BOSS, EXPULSION
70 WELLS CATHEDRAL, WEST FRONT, NOAH BUILDING THE ARK
71 OXFORD DIVINITY SCHOOL, MADONNA AND CHILD
72 BEVERLEY MINSTER REREDOS, CORONATION OF THE VIRGIN
73 EXETER BISHOP'S THRONE, HEAD OF THE CARVER
74 EXETER TRANSEPT CHAPEL, THE CRUCIFIXION

76 PRIOR SUTTON'S TOMB AT OXFORD.

75 BISHOP AQUABLANCA'S TOMB, HEREFORD, 1270

external screen is that at Exeter framing the west front (68), constructed in two tiers 1330-70, the lower figures being the earlier in date. The niches are filled with kings, bishops, knights cross-legged, vivid and lifelike, cut with the south-western feeling and technique; to these may be added the reredos at Christchurch where, although the principal figures have been destroyed, much of interest remains. The woodworkers produced figurework which they mingled with their foliage. The corbels of the bishop's throne at Exeter with the heads of the carvers (73), the stall-ends of Chester with the stem of Jesse (91) and the vaulting bosses at Ripon (69), containing figures five feet in height, depicting Scriptural scenes, and with single figures, all show the capabilities of the carpenters when they essayed the higher forms of craftsmanship.

After the Black Death the methods of production changed; owing to the shortage of masons both architectural detail and sculpture became shopwork, divorced from the local and individual masons building, and for the last 200 years altered but little in either methods or style. An exception to this statement must however be made in that the general treatment of architecture was varied by local conditions developing individual twists of thought. The same may be said of effigy making, the shopwork of London, Bristol, York and Nottingham each having their own particular methods of production and ornament.

Hundreds of empty niches testify to the mass production of figure sculpture with which they were originally filled. On the exteriors only odd figures remain, such as are to be found on the towers at Wrexham and Gresford, and the Madonna and Resurrection at Isle Abbots. Early sixteenth century work is shown at Tiverton on the Greenway chapel and porch; both Old and New Testament subjects are carved, together with a splendid series of ships with which Greenway made his patrimony (148, 149). The most numerous collection of fifteenth-century sculpture is at Westminster, in the chantry of Henry V and the chapel of Henry VII. In the range of figures in Henry VII's chapel 95 remain out of 107. The kings in the pulpitum at Canterbury (5) and the later theatrical figures in the pulpitum at York indicate the general trend of figure sculpture during the last years. The Divinity School at Oxford has many niched figures in both the east and west walls (62) and niched figures and Scriptural subjects in the bosses and pendants. The Beauchamp chapel at Warwick retains much of its lesser figurework, especially in the east window, where there is a representation of the nine orders of angels (67, 146). Fragments of statues

which once adorned the great screens at Winchester (65) and
St. Cuthbert's Wells have been recovered and many other
fragments survive. The pulpits of the south-west sometimes
have kept their images as at Bovey Tracy, Slymbridge and
Trull, as well as in screenwork at Lustleigh, Bridford and
Manaton.

The woodworkers were not afraid of figurework, although
they rarely had the accomplishment of the masons and shop-
men; these are found in bench-ends at Barkston, the Wiggenhalls (116), Combe-in-Teignhead, Haverford West and Hull,
and small figures cut on the top edge at Winchester Lady chapel,
East Barning, Norton, Enville and Ludlow. Such work occurs
in stall elbows, doorways, roofs and font-covers, and there are
reproductions of alabaster work at Coventry (64). Small images
have escaped on the Speke chapel at Exeter (61), the reredos
of the Oldham chapel and the Kirkham chantry chapel screen
at Paignton, although usually mutilated. There is a lovely
series of angel bosses in the quire vault at Gloucester (55),
together with corbel heads, which are to be found in profusion
almost in every church.

TOMB DESIGN

"Without a belief of some kind of spiritual world the artist is only half an artist . . . his love of beauty becomes of itself a spiritual belief. But what of morality, of goodness, of truth and self-sacrifice, of love for the world and the people in it? Has the artist any concern in these things? Is he less of an artist if he has?"

HUGH WALPOLE, *Roman Fountain*, page 206

IN the study of the existing memorials and tombs with which our churches are still enriched, a complete miniature history may be found not only of mediaeval architecture and the crafts, but a chronological perspective of the changes in armour and the costumes and headdresses of the ladies. In addition, it enables us to realise the growing importance of heraldry, the cult of saint worship, and the increased consideration given to the souls of the departed. Unfortunately but a tithe of the generous output in memorials escaped destruction, which was of such magnitude as to have formed the major employment of the craftsmen of the middle ages. Although the architectural setting out of tomb design, including the chest upon which the effigies were placed and the hanging canopies reared above them, varied both in design and detail with the passage of time, they continue to be of absorbing interest, only second to the sculptured effigies of which they formed the setting.

The design and execution of the memorials and tombs of the first half of our period was controlled by the master mason; after the Black Death however the quarry centres and shop gilds gradually dominated the scene independent of the mason, who in the earlier time had produced the admirable memorials we still admire. From the first the varied materials employed were as relevant in their influence on design and methods of treatment as were the changing fashions of costume and format. These materials included Purbeck and Frosterley marbles, free-stones, sandstones, chalk and Beer stone, alabaster, wood, laton and bronze; many of these including timber formed the foundations of the effigies, upon which was laid a coating of gesso, stamped in patterning with dies and afterwards painted and gilt, now unfortunately almost wholly gone.

During the twelfth and early centuries, burials inside churches were confined to ecclesiastics and abbots, the chapter-house being reserved for the latter. In the days before the Norman Conquest the bodies of the saints had been interred in crypts placed beneath the high altar; however in later days these precious relics were brought into the upper church and elevated upon shrine bases and loaded with gifts from the devout, who came to honour and also to seek indulgences. In the parish churches the founders were often interred on the north side of the chancel, placed within the wall under an arched recess. When interior burials became customary, recesses were general, as the series in Carlisle cathedral and the later set at Malpas, Cheshire. The bodies of important people were usually placed within hewn stone coffins; if these were outside the church they were buried to the lip of the coffin and surmounted by a slab with a cross either incised or carved upon it, together with a symbol of recognition; if a priest a chalice and book, if a knight a sword and shield, if a layman, his occupation such as a pair of shears, or as at York a bell for a bellfounder. Early representations of the figures were in low relief, primitive in drawing and execution; later they became more deeply cut until they stood well above the surrounding framework, as shown in the early abbots at Peterborough and bishops at Exeter. Early primitive effigies were designed as standing figures laid upon their backs and make no pretence to repose, bishops holding the staff in one hand and blessing with the other; knights with their hands resting upon the hilts of their swords, their feet standing upon an animal.

When the stone coffin was brought within the building, the sides were decorated with quatrefoils as at Llanrwst, or it was enclosed by marble slabs designed with quatrefoils containing seated figures as the tomb of Bp. Marshall (1210) at Exeter; this is an excellent example of the Purbeck school, who while at first supplying carved building materials, had later to depend on a trade in memorials. These early chest tombs set a fashion which continued till long after the suppression, although enriched in differing ways during the course of time. At York 1255 Archbp. Gray is buried under a canopied tomb similar to the shrine bases, consisting of a gabled roof standing upon a trefoiled and pillared arcade resting upon the tomb chest; this was a forerunner of canopied tomb design. Bp. Bridport 1164 at Salisbury has a two-bay canopy roofed as before, but at Hereford over the effigy of Bp. Aquablanca 1270 the roof has disappeared (75), its place being taken by steep-sided gables divided by attenuated pinnacles, the centre finial having a miniature representation of the Crucifixion. This steep gable is found in the early canopies at Westminster abbey and in the timber stalls at Lancaster (86). During this time however many foreigners were employed, and it is well to keep in mind

77 YORKSHIRE. A LADY, HAREWOOD
78 YORKSHIRE. A KNIGHT, WEST TANFIELD

79 CANTERBURY CATHEDRAL, TOMB OF THE BLACK PRINCE, 1376

that the Royal house was more French than English. The shrine of St. Edward for instance was enriched by Italians with mosaics; the tombs of Henry III and William de Valence with enamels from Limoges, as were other tombs now lost to us, such as that of Walter of Merton, bp. of Rochester 1276. The effigies of the king and his consort were cast in bronze and are of great magnificence. Canopy design may be followed at Westminster from the close of the thirteenth century into the fourteenth, in the tombs of Aveline and her husband Edmund Crouchback, together with that of William de Valence. The short period of natural foliage may be studied in the shrine bases of Saints Frideswide, Alban, and Cantelupe, and tombs at Exeter and Ely. During this time the Purbeck marblers continued to supply their memorials; they introduced the stiff leaf foliage which is used so effectively round the effigies of Bps. Northwold and Kilkenny 1254–6 at Ely. Although they still were in evidence after the close of the century, other influences were at work, and freestones were taking the place of Purbeck. These various stones altered both design and posture; the Somerset oolite was thinly bedded, and its use kept the effigy flat with head unraised; Beer stone and northern magnesian limestone on the other hand could be cut in large sizes and was easily worked. The Midlands used a soft sandstone, resulting in a coarsened cutting; however the majority of these productions received their coat of gesso, upon which the finer details were modelled and then painted and gilt.

During the first fifty years of the fourteenth century the mason was gradually losing control, as is indicated by the absence of a broadness of handling; nevertheless the work of these earlier years is of the greatest interest. The effigies are no longer designed as standing figures laid upon their backs, but are carved in natural poses, the knights with their legs crossed or in the attitude of the dying gladiator, or grasping the sword ready to spring up, or asleep, as the figure at Abergavenny. The knights at Aldworth, Chew Magna and Clehonger show a freedom of style and a vigorous grasp of life which is unusual in any other phase of mediaeval art; the cross-legged knight is a peculiarity of English style. During the earlier part cushions were placed beneath the heads of the effigies; by the middle of the century, however, the helm came into fashion for knights in armour; their pose was straightened out, their legs uncrossed, their hands no longer on their swords but clasped in prayer.

The tomb format during these fifty years is as interesting as that of the effigies. The Westminster tombs have already been mentioned—the great canopied gables were broadened out, their surfaces elaborately decorated. The tomb chest design was no longer of quatrefoils but a series of closely set niches, filled with miniature statuettes of delightful pose, representing relatives, kings, queens, knights and ladies. The recessed tomb was continued, either actually cut out or through the wall, or placed against it, forming a wall tomb. The first are found at Bristol, Ducklington, Halsall and Wingfield, those cut through the wall at Hull and Goldsborough, and those against the wall at Bredon, Winchelsea and in the chapel of St. Andrew at Exeter. During this time the plain arch and the ogee shape were interchangeable, but always becoming richer in detail and more ornate in character. In the Bristol Lady chapel, Bredon, and at Oxford (76) the ball flower is used either dotted or threaded into a twisted stem; generally however the canopies have cusped foliage, with finials and tall pinnacles, the inner tracery full and free. The Ducklington tomb recesses are enriched by the stem of Jesse springing from his body lying between the ogee arches, the whole designed as a vine interspersed with heads. Independent canopies partook of much the same character with tall gables, as that over the tomb of prior Sutton, Oxford 1320 (76), the lovely Wimbische and Cantelupe canopies at Lincoln, or the heavier and stronger type at Ottery St. Mary. A suggestion of the later forms is already visible in the tomb of Bp. Stapleton 1326 at Exeter and the Graunson tomb 1335 at Hereford, the latter composed in two horizontal stories.

The northern style had more freedom and richness and was in every sense prodigal in output and lavish in ornament, with a natural beauty about it all which saves it from vulgarity. The tombs of this school may be studied at Cartmel, Bainton, Welwick, Hull, and Beverley and are on the level of its architecture, shown in the quires of Guisborough, Ripon and Selby, the chapter-houses at Southwell and York, and the churches of Heckington, Howden and Patrington. The splendour of the canopy over the Percy tomb at Beverley (6), crowded as it is with sculpture and carving, animal, foliage, and heraldry as well as figurework, is a veritable masterpiece of the mason's and sculptor's art. The more it is examined the more amazing it becomes; every spandrel both inside and out contains its figure, be it the Deity, the Queen of Heaven, saints, angels, lords, and ladies, the whole embroidered with a magnificent and luxuriant vine trail, cusped and finialed with bulbous leaves and marvellous serrated frillings. The Harrington tomb at Cartmel is of about the same date, but is not so accomplished or masterly in technique, but contains a mass of detail, unfortunately much knocked about. The effigies are surrounded by a procession of canons chanting from their books, while below they are sat in groups singing, with one book to three canons.

Shrine format continued in various materials; at Stanton Harcourt Purbeck marble is employed; at Lincoln freestone, at Chester red sandstone. The first is crowded with detail, heads, statuettes, coats of arms and fine cusping; the shrine of St. Hugh's head at Lincoln 1350 is similar but more refined in detail. At Chester St. Werburgh's shrine has been pieced together from fragments found, and has a base and canopy, the latter full of small niches containing many Saxon kings, the ancestors of the saint, and although their heads have gone small portions of the gold and colours are visible. The shrine of St. Etheldreda at Ely is a substantial construction of considerable height; all these examples are completed above by a horizontal line. The same love of crowded niches and pinnacles above the effigy is shown over the figure of Edward II at Gloucester, and to Edward lord Spencer 1370 at Tewkesbury, which can be matched later in the canopy over Archbishop Bowett 1423 at York, and the chantry chapels of Waynfleete (80) and Beaufort at Winchester.

During this period a new medium for effigy and tomb making was introduced which was later to revolutionise the methods, construction and craft of tomb design. This material was found in abundance in the red marl of the upper Keuper beds in Derbyshire, Nottinghamshire and Staffordshire; when first quarried it is soft, but hardens on exposure and may then be polished. The principal quarries were at Chelleston and Tutbury, and the towns of Nottingham and later Burton were the distributing centres. It is first noticed in a cross-legged effigy at Hanbury in Staffordshire 1300 and was also used in the construction of the western portal of Tutbury priory. It was employed for the tombs of Edward II at Gloucester, his son lord John of Eltham, Queens Philippa and Isabel (the latter destroyed) and the little princes at Westminster and William their brother at York. Other fine examples include Bp. John Hotham 1337 at Ely; Bp. Ralph of Shrewsbury 1363 at Wells; Thomas Beauchamp 1370 at Warwick; Archbp. Langham 1376 at Westminster, and Bp. John Harewell 1386 at Wells. This alabaster rapidly became the principal medium for important and fashionable tomb-making.

From this time onwards the pose of the figure and its setting out altered but little, for the age of experiment was over, and tomb design was in the hands of the shop trade, who although accomplished craftsmen, seemed to have had little initiative, and were content to continue the production of the same class of effigy and tomb from father to son until the work became more hackneyed and trite with each decade. The pose of the knight is a rigid one, the head on a helm, the feet upon an animal, the legs straight, the body forming a slight arc; the lady with cushioned head and attendant angels as at Ewelme, both holding their hands in prayer when not clasping each others' hands. A feature of this type is the "gablette" or canopy at the head of the effigy, of which fine examples are at Lowick on the Green tomb, the duchess of Suffolk at Ewelme, Thomas earl of Arundel and his countess at Arundel, and Henry IV and Queen Joan at Canterbury. The special decoration of the tomb chest from the Chelleston centre was the introduction of angel weepers bearing shields, standing upon pedestals under tabernacled niches. In the York type two angels hold a shield between them as at Swine and Harewood, or a single sprightly little angel resting upon one knee steadies the shield in position as at Methley and Harewood. Relations and saints continued to occupy the niches, as in the fine series round the Boteler tomb at Warrington; later, bedesmen stand round the tombs of their benefactors, as at Arundel, and at North Ashton, Oxon. In the early years of the sixteenth century niches tend to disappear, the alabaster men copying the glaziers and grouping the relations, the children kneeling behind their respective parents; an early example of this method is an alabaster slab to a Gylbert at Youlgreave 1492; at Ross on Wye the arms and mantling come between the family and a representation of the Holy Trinity, and at St. Michael Coventry the arms occupy the centre as a foundation to the crucifix.

The canopy design of the fifteenth century differed from what had gone before in being completed by a horizontal cresting in place of the gable, but this did not alter the use of a complexity of architectural forms in their construction; the four-centred or flattened Tudor arch is common at Bristol St. Mark, York, Great Brington, Lincoln, Exeter and St. Mary Redcliffe, Long Ashton, Edington and Colyton, often with demi-angels. The semicircular arch is employed at Methley, and a close-set acutely pointed gable with upright tracery is found at Southwark and St. Bartholomew's Smithfield. The Wakeman cenotaph at Tewkesbury is completed by three canopied niches in imitation of stallwork. Many of these stone canopies are extremely elegant and rich; those in the Lady chapel at Exeter placed over earlier effigies of bishops, the two at St. Mark's, Bristol, to sir Thomas Berkeley and abbot Salley with delicate lacework headings, the lovely canopy over sir Richard Choke at Long

80 WINCHESTER CATHEDRAL, CARDINAL BEAUFORT'S CHANTRY CHAPEL

LONDON ALABASTER WORK SHOWING REMAINS OF COLOUR DECORATION

Ashton with demi-angels, and the magnificent tomb at Ewelme over the duchess of Suffolk are all examples of finely designed and technically excellent production.

The important development of the chantry chapel during the fifteenth century produced many and varied forms of this architectural addition to the churches. A chantry did not of necessity mean a chapel but a priest, nevertheless a chapel added greatly to its dignity and importance; this could be in the form of a structural addition to the building, or the enclosure of some part of the original church, fenced off by screenwork either in stone or timber, its size proportionate to its dignity. Nearly every church in the land had at least one chantry chapel, while abbeys and cathedrals had many, kings, abbots, bishops, and squires vying with each other in producing the richest and most perfect tomb-house, and verily some of them are truly magnificent. When we review the chapels of Alcock and West (4, 35) at Ely, Speke and Oldham at Exeter, Waynfleete (80), Beaufort, Fox and Gardner at Winchester, Sugar and Bubwith at Wells, Warwick and Despencer at Tewkesbury, Ramryge's at St. Albans, Bird's at Bath, Prince Arthur's at Worcester, to name only a few, all of them surrounded by ornate stone screens, with elaborately vaulted roofs, the chapels filled without and within by canopied niches once occupied by statuary, the majority of them still retaining the alabaster tombs and effigies of the dignitaries for whom they were built, each with its enriched altar and reredos, we realise how much this notable development of the chantry chapel meant both to the craftsmen and the gild shops of the time.

The most resplendent chantry chapel is that of Henry VII at Westminster forming a great Lady chapel, but there are others so tiny as to leave barely room for the priest to stand. They were sometimes placed in unusual positions, as the suspended chapel of Henry V approached by spiral staircases, forming a canopy over the king's monument beneath, and decorated by tiers of niched figures and heraldry, the whole said to have been designed by the king himself. In general design however the chantry chapel was surrounded by screenwork, panelled below, with open tracery above, as at Warwick, Exeter, Bath, Winchester and Worcester. This resemblance in the sixteenth century was often taken a step further by the addition of a second storey designed as a gallery front; this is found at Exeter in the Speke and Oldham Chapels, at Westminster in abbot Islip's chapel and the feature was also used for tombs, as the one at St. Katherine's Hospital to the duke of Somerset 1447, and at Yatton to sir John Newton 1487. Two storeys are found at St. Albans in the chapel of abbot Ramryge 1520 and tomb of Humphrey duke of Gloucester. Exaggerated height is shown in the chapels of Wykeham at Winchester and the Warwick chapel at Tewkesbury. Nichework, gables and pedestals predominate in the Waynfleete and Beaufort chapels at Winchester and the Kirkham chapel at Paignton, as formerly they did at Tiverton; at Ely the divisional walls are in the solid, the admittance through doorways, the Alcock chapel crowded with the stone-cutter's version of canopied stallwork, the West chapel having more than a touch of Italian renaissance in its enrichments.

Even in a rapid survey of tomb design during the middle ages one is struck not only by the thought and care bestowed upon monumental art, but the infinite variety and diversity of design, combined with the ingenuity displayed in their construction and enrichment. It is this diversity and opulence which has been the cause of so much disparaging criticism from those steeped in the staid classicism of Greece, who cannot understand the urge which produced such rapid changes in form and detail without losing anything of its vitality. One might speak even of its explosive character, taking fire at a hint and constantly producing fresh combinations as it took its course for nearly four hundred years.

ALABASTER PANELS

THAT the alabaster quarry centres did not confine themselves to work of a monumental nature is evident by the numbers of small tables or panels of religious subjects scattered over the continent; many fragments have also been dug up in England, in spite of two hundred years of iconoclasm; they seem to have been popular both for private as well as public devotions. At the suppression the inventories then taken show a surprising number of alabaster tables or reredoses which were to be sold or otherwise destroyed. Many of these went across the seas where there were already considerable numbers distributed in France, Germany, and as far as Iceland. These small panels could be conveyed with little trouble and assembled together in the form of a reredos upon reaching their destination. Sir William Hope shows that a large alabaster reredos from Nottingham was erected in 1367–9 in the chapel of the Order of the Garter at Windsor for the enormous sum of £200. The Nevill reredos at Durham, erected in 1380, was adorned with magnificent images in alabaster including "Our Lady standinge in the midst, and the picture of St. Cuthbert on the one side and the picture of St. Oswald on the other, beinge all richly gilded." The principal centre of distribution of these panels was Nottingham, although plain slabs were supplied from the quarries to other centres, principally London and York, where they were carved.

These essentially pictorial subjects, vigorously cut and brilliantly painted, were also in use in the decoration of the sides of the alabaster tombs for which the Chelleston and Tutbury quarries were celebrated. The saints decorating the tomb at Warrington, St. George, St. Christopher; St. Michael weighing the souls at Harewood, the Madonna and Child and the Holy Trinity on the tombs at Willoughby, the delightful Annunciation and Trinity at Wells and the Madonna and Child at Minster Lovel are in the same class as those of the panelled tables or reredos. The earliest tablets and small figures date from the middle of the fourteenth century, and from that time their production constantly increased until the suppression. At first they are of a quality comparable to fourteenth century figure sculpture, as the lovely St. Barbara with her cannon ball now in the V. and A. museum, and the Nativity from Long Melford (82). A well-known type belonging to the last years of

H

the century and the early years of the next is completed above
with an embattled cornice bayed upwards and forwards; these
panels are about 15 inches in height and 11 in breadth (83). The
costumes alter but little with the passage of time; there was
not the same necessity to keep abreast of fashion as in the effigies
for a tomb, for these panels of religious subjects treated pictorially had little need of fashions. The soldiers represented in
the popular subject of the Resurrection wear a sharp-pointed
basinet which may be dated about 1380, a loose jupon, bawdrick,
the lower limbs encased in plate armour which they continued
to wear from one type to the next.

The series from 1420–60 are without embattled heads, having
separate canopies, gabled and delicately traceried as at Lydiate,
Lancashire. They were used in the construction of the great
retables, and were purposely left rough edged. The popular
sets include the Passion and the B.V.M. The first embraced the
Betrayal, Flagellation, Crucifixion, Entombment, Resurrection,
Bearing and Descent from the Cross, Christ before Pilate and
the Last Supper. The B.V.M. set included the Annunciation (85),
Gifts of the Kings, Adoration, Assumption, Coronation (83),
Salutation, Nativity, Circumcision, and Ascension. Other
groups illustrated the Martyrdom of St. Katherine, St. Thomas
of Canterbury, the legends of many other saints, as well as a
set depicting the Last Judgment. These however formed but
a small proportion of the many subjects which were carved,
such as the *Te Deum* series, St. Edmund and other martyrdoms,
including St. Erasmus; the carving of narrow panels containing
upright figures for placing between subject panels of a retable
were common. For examples of the complete reredos either
single, two tiered or in the form of a tryptych we have to go
to such places as Bordeaux, Montreal, La Celle, Compiègne,
Yssac le Tourelle, Amiens and other churches in France. All
these panels were coloured and gilt, the foreground green,
spotted with red and white daisies, the background with gilt
knobs in the style of the mediaeval painters. The garments were
coloured with narrow borders, the haloes gilt, as was the hair
of the saints and martyrs, who wore placid white faces and
mild eyes in contrast to the reprobates and tormentors with
tawny rugged features and black hair. The mystery plays of the
fifteenth century were a mine of detail for the carvers, as they
were for the sculptors and glassworkers; the grouping of the
figures and their dress reflect what the craftsman had seen for
himself when watching the property angels and soldiers during
the Whitweek representations.

As we have seen in regard to the Durham reredos, the

82 LONG MELFORD, SUFFOLK, ALABASTER PANEL OF THE ADORATION

VARYING TYPES OF ALABASTER PANELWORK USED IN MAKING A REREDOS

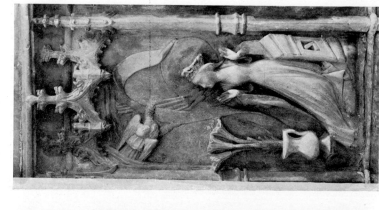

85 THE ANNUNCIATION
WELLS CATHEDRAL

84 ST. WILFRED
RIPON CATHEDRAL

83 THE CORONATION OF THE VIRGIN
RIPON CATHEDRAL

alabaster workers produced large figures independently of the
panels. In 1779 three were found under the church floor at
Flawford, Notts—the B.V.M. and St. Peter 32 inches in height
and a bishop over three feet, all of excellent pose. At Beauchief
abbey was found a large panel illustrating the martyrdom of
St. Thomas of Canterbury, and there are technically fine figures
at Lydiate of St. Cuthbert and at Ripon though smaller that of
St. Wilfred (84). In St. Mary's hall Coventry* were wooden
imitations of alabaster figures, including a fine St. George on
horseback killing a dragon (64), and six other subjects which
owe their design to the alabaster workers, and so we find once
again craftsmen copying each other's format in a different
medium.

* Now destroyed.

THE WORK OF THE CARPENTER AND CARVER

"... Art is the one achievement of man which, as far as in him lies
has been consistently faithful to the profoundest of his incentives,
and in a world of the transitory is surest of preservation. ... Even
if craftsmanship may in part be learned, no art can be taught and
none of any fine purpose deliberately imitated."
WALTER DE LA MARE, *Pleasures and Speculations*, 156

IF the thirteenth century may be said to have been the age of
the figure sculptor and the fourteenth that of the stone carver,
the fifteenth may certainly be assigned to the woodworker,
whose output is its chief claim to fame above that accomplished
by any other craftsmanship during the period. Before that
time however it may be said with truth that he failed either to
assert the dignity of his craft or to demand the prerogatives of
his material, for, during the earlier time he was dominated by
the mason, working in his way and using timber as stone, with
no natural aptitude for the qualities of wood or instinct for its
inherent possibilities, dowelling his stuff together without
grasping the value of mortice and tenon. Very little of his
early work survives, and its interest lies chiefly in showing the
early clumsy methods compared with his later genius, lacking
as it does either beauty of proportion or charm of detail. His
decorative motifs were culled from the same source, using the
arcade either simply or trefoiled as it appears on chests, tombs,
and screens; when he comes before us in the thirteenth century
he is completely in thrall to masons' methods. This is shown in
the screen at Stanton Harcourt, Oxon, with the tracery cut out
of thick horizontal planking, the heads of trefoil shape carefully
moulded with an additional weather mould planted above them,
the whole of this resting upon thin turned circular shafts with
caps, annulets, and moulded bases as in stonework. The same
methods are employed in portions of screenwork remaining
in Yorkshire at Beverley St. Mary, Kirk Ella, and Ripley and
at Long Itchington in Warwickshire. This imitation of fourteenth century masons' mouldings must have taxed all the
resources of the carpenters of the time, with the tracery a replica
of that used for windows, and moulded in much the same way.
The doorway at Kirk Ella is a careful copy in wood of a piece
of mason-craft, resembling the main exterior doorway of a
church, with three columns capped and based on either side of
the deep arch, with mouldings to match. The chests of the time

52

86 LANCASTER, STALLWORK NORTH SIDE OF QUIRE

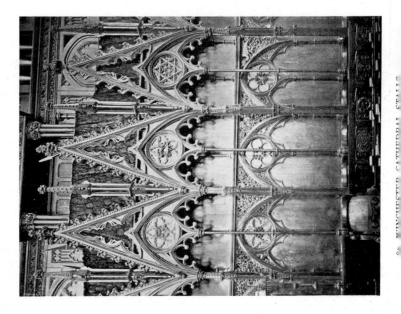

SHOWING THE DEVELOPMENT OF CANOPY-WORK FROM STONE IDEALS TO WOOD

WINCHESTER CATHEDRAL STALLS

EXAMPLES OF THE WORK OF THE RIPON CARVERS. THE BROMFLETS

90 RIPON STALLWORK, CANOPY OVER STALL

89 MANCHESTER STALLWORK, STALL END

91 CHESTER CATHEDRAL, THE DEAN'S STALL END IN QUIRE, 1380

are constructed of slabs of timber dowelled together and
clamped with ironwork; a little earlier they had been dug out
from a solid trunk, as is the pulpit at Mellor. Chests were
enriched in various ways; often the smith took on the work
with twisted scrollwork, or if by the woodworker, designs in
chip carving at Earl Stonham, Suffolk and All Saints, Hereford,
or with more elaboration at Brailes or Munslow. As he advanced
he produced the rich but shallowly carved fronts at Hacconby
and Wath. Turned shafts were still in use at the commencement
of the fourteenth century, and are employed in the screens at
St. Margaret, King's Lynn; Chichester Hospital; Wolfhamcote
Warwick; Southacre Norfolk, but at Thame the shafting has
become octagonal; with the exception of Southacre the tracery
remains massive and heavy.

As the fourteenth century advanced, the woodworkers and
carvers attempted marvellous translations from stone to wood,
incredibly difficult and wonderfully clever, but entirely wrong-
headed and wasteful both in labour and time; it is however
impossible not to admire the finer examples of this mistaken
craft and give it notice. The screenwork in Chichester Hospital
and at St. Margaret, King's Lynn has imitation stone tracery
with astonishing leaf carving in the cuspings, and the same may
be said of Southacre. The stalls at Chichester and the screen at
Lavenham have open ogee heads with bulbous foliaged cusps
and finials. The earliest remaining stallwork is at Winchester (87),
the design an elaborate version of the Chichester Hospital
screen; it is planned as a two-bay scheme; the panelling behind
the seating is decorated with blind window tracery, the spandrels
between enriched with wonderful foliage interspersed with
armed knights, dragons, monkeys and other conceits. The
designer of this work, Master Thomas of Winton, had also a
hand in the bishop's throne erected at Exeter in 1312, with a
canopy rising sixty feet and spiring into the quire vault, including pedestals for six images for which the carver was paid 32s.,
Master Thomas coming to choose the timber and no doubt
providing the design. The carving of the vine trails growing
up the ogee arches is as splendid as that in stone on the Percy
tomb at Beverley: a cusp carved with a virile man's head is
probably that of the carver Robert Galmeton, who received
four pounds for his labours (73). The woodwork of the throne
would originally be painted and gilt with the addition of gesso
and glass mosaics, very sumptuous in appearance.

Perhaps the most exciting work is the stalls now at Lancaster (86), probably forty years later than those at Winchester;
they are a glorified version of the former, this time however a

one-bay design with tall attenuated gabled canopies divided by pinnacled standards encrusted with ornament. Nowhere out of France is to be found such a wealth of flamboyant tracery design, not only in the heads of the ogee arches, but inside each tapering gable the flowing tracery runs riot: wherever a surface offers its opportunity to the carver he enriched it with tracery which is rarely duplicated. Along the upper edge of each ogee and gable is a continuous cresting of natural foliage, the gables and pinnacles completed with knops of leafage. The mouldings used have accentuated deep hollows almost enclosed, which could be manipulated in stone but presented almost insuperable difficulties in wood; the woodmen surmounted them by making the hollows come at the edge of each plank, half on each side, which were then dowelled together in a primitive way, and have nevertheless outlasted many more finely constructed materials. The fronts of both sets are on one plane without any attempt at breaking the line. The use of the masons' formulas is illustrated both at Winchester and Lancaster: the former a close copy of the stone canopies, as the one over the tomb of Bp. Peter of Aquablanca (1270) at Hereford (75), the latter from the side gables of the canopy over the tomb of Edmund Crouchback (died 1296) at Westminster, just as a hundred and fifty years later the mason was to copy the wood-worker in the canopywork of the Warwick chapel (1422) at Tewkesbury and the decoration of Bp. Alcock's chapel (1500) at Ely (35) which was transcribed from the northern stallwork of the period.

The design of the seating seems to have been of long tradition; there are fragments of seating at Westminster and Salisbury enriched with dog-tooth and the trefoiled lily leaf, and there are other early examples at Etchingham, Sussex, and Anstey, Herts; also at Great Budworth, Cheshire, Weston-in-Gardano Nr. Bristol, and Hemingborough, Yorks, as well as early misericords at Exeter. The more important sets had always canopies and there are a few shafts at Peterborough with trefoil foliaged caps from the now destroyed stalls: we also know from Sandford that the thirteenth century stalls at Westminster had acutely pointed arches supported upon slender turned shafts.

Gradually however the carpenter was coming to his own, and with such exceptions as the Tewkesbury stalls, his technique improved; at Ely about the same date as Lancaster we find the actual inception of the final stall design; it is in two storeys, the lower canopies over the seating separated from the upper tier by horizontal mouldings, the upper set with spires,

92 WOODBRIDGE, SUFFOLK
FONT COVER

93 EDLESBOROUGH, BUCKS
PULPIT

which though short appear as part of the design; the general front, however, remained upon one plane. At Hereford in the cathedral and at All Saints a further step was taken in that the ogee-shaped canopies of the arches are bowed forward in front of the shafting, and a little later at Gloucester (88) the efforts at Ely and Hereford are used in combination, although as yet the spires are not freed but framed within a traceried screen: it is however not a far cry from Gloucester to Lincoln, where in 1370 the woodcraftsman showed his completed scheme, which was never to be bettered.

Before he arrived at this stage of transition two other works call for attention, both of them in Beverley Minster, the sedilia and the quire screens, the latter the earlier of the two; they both adopt the bowing ogee in front of a gable, unsuitable for screenwork but admirable for sedilia, nevertheless they are amazing efforts in craftsmanship, the earlier having natural, the latter bulbous foliage; here again they lack the coloured and gilt gesso with which they were originally enriched. For a time the woodworker continued in a modified form his use of masons' mouldings, improving however in his construction, ceasing to cut through his vertical standards and strengthening thereby the rigidity of his framework. Many fourteenth century screens are pleasant in their proportions and exciting in their flamboyant tracery: at Lavenham with superimposed straight-sided gables, at Holme, Hale and Mattishall in Norfolk, and Grundisburgh in Suffolk they form a series of interesting compositions, the craftsmen discarding the early clumsy and heavy methods exemplified in the pulpit at Fulbourne, Cambridge for the real right thing.

The year 1370 marks the full entrance of the woodworker into his kingdom; although no longer subordinate to the mason he continued to make use of his decorative formulas, transfusing into them however something light, soaring and delicate: in fact he had become wood-conscious, and the sinew or grain of his material was from now to be a help and not a hindrance in his work. His output became full of interest and significance both in the technical skill displayed in his construction of roofs, decorated doors and porches but especially in his stalls, screens and furniture. It is however in the examination of the canopied stallwork that his genius may perhaps be best appreciated. The existing sets commencing with Lincoln continue with Chester, Nantwich, Whalley, Carlisle, Ripon, Manchester and Beverley: these however form but a small part of the output of stallwork in the north; there is indubitable evidence of sets at Bridlington, Durham, Jervaulx, Roche, and York: other noble churches had their sets such as Byland, Bolton, Cartmel, Combermere, Fountains, Furness, Kirkstall, Meaux, Rievaulx, and Vale Royal. It is pitiable to know that many sets, completed within fifty years of the suppression, were at once smashed to pieces and utterly destroyed by the contemptuous officials of a government whose mind was filled with possible gain to the king but positive gain to themselves.

The splendid spiring stalls of which Lincoln is now our earliest example is the intuition of the northern craftsmen, and is not to be found in perfection elsewhere; even the sets at Windsor and Henry VII's chapel have little in common with this admirable design and even finer execution, the sole result of northern genius. If the output of the Yorkshire carvers be compared with the work in Somerset and Devon its superiority is at once apparent; it is cleaner cut, more faultless in design, less fussy and confusing, stronger and more restrained. During the time the latest sets were under construction they remained essentially English, whereas the south of England had succumbed to alien fashions shown in the stallwork at Christchurch, Hants; Henry VII's chapel at Westminster and even the earlier set at Windsor, all of which mark a rapid change in outlook and approach, and have little connection with English tradition.

The Lincoln design is in two storeys, the lower canopies over the seating having three sides on plan with connecting pinnacles at each angle, every face having a bowing ogee set before a tall gable, all cusped and finialed. These canopies are completed above by a moulded brattishing, upon which stand the two-sided niches with gablets and pinnacles above, completed by tall and slender cusped and finialed spires which are flanked by attenuated pinnacled standards the niches connected to them by flat open tracery. The general effect is very lovely, the upper storey perhaps a little thin and open. There may have been intermediate designs now lost to us: if not, Lincoln is an astonishing development from Hereford and Gloucester. Ten years later the Chester set was erected, the Lincoln conception glorified: ogee archlets are placed in front of the little gables, the upper niches become three-sided in place of two, and their canopies are miniature reproductions of the ones below; the spires remain as slender as before but the dividing pinnacled standards are shorter. In the rich tabernacle carving placed round the pulpitum three spired niches are crowded over each lower canopy, giving a wonderful sense of complexity. At Nantwich (1390) stall design reaches a high water-mark. The two-storied conception of Lincoln and Chester is for the moment abandoned and the design becomes a harmonious

97 KENTISBERE SCREEN, DEVON

WELSH TYPE COMPARED WITH THE WORK OF THE BROMFLET CARVERS OF RIPON

99 JESUS CHAPEL SCREEN, MANCHESTER

98 PARTRISHOW SCREEN GALLERY

whole. The lower canopies have the Lincoln feeling, but the craftsman's inspiration is now devoted to the upper tier: in place of the single niche backed by flat traceried panels, three six-sided niches are grouped together, the centre one rising above the others, the capping a forest of gables and pinnacles. The result is admirable and completely satisfying. From this date however stall design reverted to the two-tier motif, which became constant and was more accentuated in the succeeding sets at Carlisle 1433, Ripon 1494 (90), and at Manchester (9) and Beverley.

The Whalley set, rescued incomplete from the abbey church at the suppression and now in the parish church, only shows us the lower canopies with their vaulting but the dividing standards remain to give data as to their original height. The abbey quire was erected between 1418 and 1434, the construction of the set being between these dates. Here is a recrudescence of the turned shafting for the lower standards, but it is now of massive proportions, which were continued to the close of the period. Carlisle is without the archlets in the lower canopies but the upper tier has three niches, each of two sides with small spires set in front of the main spire, forming a happy combination; the pulpitum is richly decorated but simple as compared with Chester.

The question is often asked who produced this magnificently vital stuff, and with Ripon 1494 (90) we are able to say with some certainty that it was the result of shopwork and craft gilds. York possessed an excellent centre in the firm of Drawswerd, a business carried on for at least three generations, the best-known member being Thomas, who was chamberlain of the city 1501, sheriff 1505–6, alderman 1508, member of Parliament 1511–12, lord mayor twice—1515 and 1523. He was a prominent craftsman in images, screens and church furniture, and is thought to have been responsible for the screens in Newark church 1508; he competed also for the tomb of Henry VII at Westminster. Thanks to Mr. J. S. Purvis we now know that there was another important centre at Ripon, where the Carver family, alias Bromflet, carried out important contracts, not only in Ripon but at Bridlington which is documented, and at Flamborough, Jervaulx, Manchester and Wensley from analytical comparison, in which the analogue is startlingly complete. Apart from Ripon (90) which contained the spire motif, their principal contribution to canopy design was to diminish the importance of the spire and enclose the whole of the stallwork under a tester, reverting back to the earlier design at Gloucester; this they proceeded to do at Manchester 1506 (9), Bridlington 1519 and Beverley 1520–4.

I

Even at Ripon the tester motif is complete over the niches placed against the end of the eastern stalls, intended for statues and wholly delightful (94). More prominence was given to the division of the tiers, the canopied detail becoming ever more intricate, with richer canopies placed over the seats of the principal ecclesiastics. During these later years there is no falling away in technique or the quality of the carving, but little essentially new is to be found in their work.

The desk standards of these stalls embody the finest designs and carving of all benching, and again the more interesting emanate from the northern centres with their magnificent front-edge buttressing (89). The shaft or cover-tree rises through a traceried base cut out of the solid, proceeding through a small gabled porch standing upon four pillars with crocketted gables and a roof decorated with little tiles and delicate eave mouldings. Above this the covertree is perforated by tiny traceries and supports a battled platform upon which is placed a little beast whose hinder legs rest easily upon the curved mouldings of the stall-end, surely the most delightful of conceits. The popeys are superb with crinkled grape foliage and bunches of fruit hanging inside and below the leaves. The face side of the standards have either tracery with shields of arms, monograms or figures standing under canopies. There is a suggestion of buttressing in many East Anglia (115-17) bench-ends but nowhere is it carried to the perfection found in the standards from Bridlington, Jervaulx, Manchester (89), Ripon and Wensley, all of which were the work of the Bromflet firm at Ripon. Other rather similar standards are at Durham castle from Bishop Auckland, and at Barkston, Leicester from some great abbey. There are marvellous standards of earlier date at Chester (91), the dean's stall carved with the stem of Jesse and the Coronation of the Virgin, not only cut on the face side but carried up the mouldings.

Bench-ends generally may be divided into two classes, those with popeys and those without, the latter often having a horizontal top; the first are to be found principally on the eastern side of England, the squared type in the west. The diversity of design, shape, mouldings and carving are endless, varying from district to district, charming and bizarre, refined and coarse, delicate and rough at the dictates of the carver, governed by his capacity for the work in hand. All motifs were employed, tracery, nichework, figures, coats of arms, foliage, genre, inscriptions and even plain sides. The benching of East Anglia has popeys and in many instances simple buttressing with platforms for animals and scenes, nearly every bench in

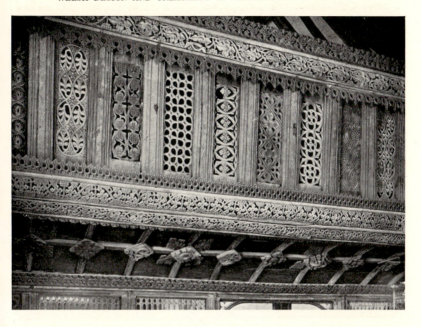

100 LLANEGRYN, SCREEN, EAST SIDE OF GALLERY, MERIONETHSHIRE
101 LLANANNO SCREEN, COVING AND DOORHEAD, RADNORSHIRE

102-4 ATHERINGTON, DEVON   105-6 LLANANNO, RADNOR
107 TONG, SALOP

many churches being decorated. Fine sets are found at Barning-
ham, Dennington and Fressingfield (117) in Suffolk and the
Wiggenhalls (116) and Walsoken with figures in Norfolk, the
majority of churches having their complement of lovely carving.
Again in the west it would be invidious to attempt a selection
from the hundreds of bench-ends in Somerset, Devon and
Cornwall, crowded as they are in almost every church, upon
them every imaginable subject finds a place and many profitable
hours may be spent upon their examination and elucidation
(112–14).

Apart from stalls, screenwork formed the major output of
the furniture executed by the fifteenth century craftsmen, for
this work had not attained full development before that time.
Few churches were without this adjunct necessary to worship,
and for fencing-off purposes, and there was ample scope for
the display of fertile talent and ingenious hands. The main
screen included a Rood-loft floor of some considerable width,
fenced on either side by gallery fronts decorated in many
ways. Beneath, the floor of the loft was either a soffit, a cove,
or latterly a lierne or fan vault, the upper part of the Rood-
screen forming its principal attraction, upholding as it did the
Rood and attendant figures, often supported by a painted
Doom as a background. Unfortunately gallery fronts, for
obvious reasons suffered an almost complete extinction at the
suppression, but some idea may be formed of their shape and
decoration by the few extant in spite of mutilation and decay.
The lovely niche scheme exhibited at Flamborough (96), Hexham and Atherington (95) and in a rougher way at Llananno
and Llanrwst give some measure of their capabilities; more
ordinary traceried fronts at Avebury, Compton Bassett, Winchester Lady chapel, Cotes-by-Stow and Sutton-on-Trent and
the more diverse tracery found at Parrishow (98), Llangwm
Uchaf, Llanegryn (100) and Llanwnog, together with the
remains of the painted saints at Strensham, all show the many
differing means employed to enrich and to give value to this
most important part of church furniture.

In the fifteenth century woodwork partook with other
crafts in the vernacular twist given by different districts to the
current style. These may be roughly divided into four main
districts; East Anglia, distinctly influenced from the continent;
the south-west, a purely local type with a touch here and there
from Brittany and Spain; Wales, this last peculiarly suited to
the simple rough and solidly built small churches which lie
scattered in the valleys of the rather wild and sombre mountain-
ous country of the Principality; finally the Northern and

Midland types, which remained essentially English. The East
Anglia types show a general tendency towards height, lightness
and grace, partly owing to the buildings in which they were
placed. The bay divisions are narrow, the tracery in their heads
often diminished to a mere fringe of cresting set on both sides
of the arch, the vaulting is small; the delicacy of the carving
and its feathery character, and the well drawn and painted
figures in the lower panelling, with the use of gesso beneath
the paint and gilt (130), give an impression of refinement and
dignity, although perhaps the detail is too diminutive in scale
to tell at a distance. Unfortunately but one or two galleries
survive; that at Attleborough shows further refinements in
niche and vaulting.

In the south-west the screenwork dominated the building,
extending as it did across the entire church. The fabrics without
clerestories are fairly low but have wide aisles, and the screenwork follows the building in being low, strong and a little
heavy; the bay divisions are wide, filled with four-light tracery
similar to the aisle windows, the lierne vaulting springing well
down and forming a prominent feature of the whole (97). The
work shows boundless energy and resourcefulness, but is
inclined to be rather rough in execution, lacking in discrimination, frustrating the aim of decoration by its very abundance;
every inch of timber is sometimes utilised. The painting of the
panelled saints is inferior to that of East Anglia, but, if we
consider the mass of work originally accomplished in this
district, it is enough to take away one's breath.

The Welsh screen design is rectangular, and vaulting is the
exception, the usual scheme being a soffit or coving as the case
may demand. The screen work is unusually low, and depended
for its effect upon the galleries, of which fortunately there are
almost as many examples left as in all the rest of England put
together. The carving is more freely designed, often each
tracery head differing in character; there are many types of
foliage, and a tracery head at Llanrwst depicts small pigs
enjoying the acorns from the oak which forms the tracery.
Ordinary tracery rarely keeps to a strict design, but is full of
quips and oddities, and in the trails the Welsh dragons disport
themselves. The whole effect is produced by a lingering Celtic
tradition adapted to mediaeval usage.

The Northern and Midland screenwork shows much variation
in design and detail, so that it is difficult to state which really
forms the type. The lovely two-bay designs with two lights
under an ogee head cusped and finialed, with rich vine trails
and elaborate crestings, found at Wensley, Flamborough, and
Manchester (99) denote the Ripon school; there are however many

individual designs; at Campsall in Yorkshire and Mobberley in Cheshire are two identical sister screens having little affinity to other work and erected in 1500. The screens at Astbury, Cheshire, and Hughley, Salop, are closely related, and although there are similarities at Gresford and Aymestry they form a small individual group, and this thing may be paralleled elsewhere. It is impossible to deal in any detail with the marvellous variety of work shown in different parts of the country, but it does show the unique capabilities of the wood craftsmen of England.

The canopied spire, cusped and pinnacled, was employed upon font covers and pulpit testers in addition to being the chief glory of stallwork; it was also used over the tomb of cardinal Kemp 1452 at Canterbury, complete with tester, and over the quire pulpit at Winchester and the lovely pulpit at Edlesborough, Bucks (93); it is however in the font covers that its suitability is apparent. From its simplest form at Wingfield and Pinchbeck, through the many varied charms of Ashbocking, Finningham, Copdock, Woodbridge (92) and Barking all in Suffolk, to the spiring beauties of Esling, Sudbury St. Gregory, Hepworth, Worlingworth and Frieston, on to the Yorkshire types at Thirsk, Bradford and Halifax, as well as further north at Newcastle, no two examples exactly alike and all interesting, until we come to the final triumphs of Ewelme and Ufford, the latter rising 18 feet above the lip of the font, would form in themselves a subject for a paper; the ingenuity displayed is extraordinary, and there would seem to be no limit as to what could be achieved by imagination, time and labour.

THE FONT COVER, UFFORD, SUFFOLK

Many efforts during the last fifty years were made by the court favourites to import fashions from the continent, were they Italian, French or Flemish, and some of this work has come down to us, largely English in construction, overlaid with foreign ornament culled from the latest books of the day; such details are found in Devon on the screenwork at Atherington, Lapford (10), Marwood, Morchard Bishop and Walkleigh, and in Somerset at Pilton. It is also found in two churches near Hereford, Foy and Llandinabo. This does not apply to the stallwork at Windsor 1477–83, Henry VII's chapel at Westminster 1509 or Christchurch, Hants, 1502–20, these being of Flemish design, even when as at Windsor the craftsmen employed were English, though under Flemish control. Other foreign designs are the stalls at King's College, Cambridge 1531 which are Italian, the screens in Winchester and St. Cross and the Salkeld screen at Carlisle 1542, this last French through Scotland, which had already influenced border woodwork as the screenwork at Hexham. All this work is divergent from English tradition, and when we consider that the Windsor stalls were constructed before Ripon, and that Westminster and Christchurch are contemporary with Manchester, it will at once be seen how far this southern woodwork was in opposition to the thought, outlook and execution of the excellent English tradition.

Something has already been said concerning the work of firms and gilds in the production of stalls and screens and a further note in regard to lesser work is not without interest. The destroyed screen at Yatton which contained 69 images was the work of the local joiner J. Crosse, who took eight years to complete his job, 1447–55. The screen at Lydd, Kent 1519–28 was however by a firm named Bellamy of Canterbury; at Hackington nearby a Hythe man named Bourversall made the screen in 1519. At Stratton in Cornwall the work was entrusted to two men, John Dawe of Lawhitton Cornwall and John Pares of North Lew Devon 1531–9. The carving of Pilton screen in Devon was given to a firm in Exeter. The erection of a screen was a lengthy job, for the timber was usually bought by the wardens as it stood, and had then to be felled and seasoned. The bench-ends at Tintinhull 1511 were made in the parish, the timber felled and cut locally. The question of timber supply is interesting; the majority of the work was executed in English oak, but foreign was also imported, the kind known as Baltic or "Danske" and referred to as "wanescot" being used for particular work, as it was sent over free from knots. In the examination of mediaeval woodwork this gives a clue as to its origin. In 1491 the wardens of Bodmin entered into a contract for the new seating of the church and a pulpit, to be completed

110 HILLESDEN, BUCKS, MIDDLE RAIL ENRICHMENT
111 BRATOFT, LINCS, PANEL TRACERY

108 CRESTING, TATTERSHALL, LINCS
109 TRACERY, TATTERSHALL, LINCS

TYPICAL SQUARE-HEADED BENCH-ENDS OF THE SOUTH-WEST OF ENGLAND

112 NORTON FITZWARREN 113 BROOMFIELD 114 LANGSTON

in four years at a cost of £92, the parish providing the timber as in the earlier roofing of the same church, when the wealthier inhabitants had given trees from their estates for this purpose.

The question of the provenance and spread of local types may perhaps be answered in the way so many parishes set about providing for a new screen. The Yatton wardens visited Easton-in-Gardano, Frome, Bitton and Selwood before deciding upon the model to follow. At Stratton it was decided that the screen should be like that at St. Kew, the Rood like Liskeard, and the Rood windows like St. Mary Weke. The stone screen at Totnes was ordered to be a copy of that before the Lady chapel at Exeter. At old St. Mary Cambridge the front of the screen was to be like that at Thriplow and the back a copy of Gasseley. In 1519 the canons of Ripon bargained for a St. George and the Dragon to be like that at Kirkstall abbey. Melrose in 1414 ordered their stalls from Bruges, the construction to be like Dunis and the carving like Thosan. Amiens stalls 1509 were to be designed from Beauvais and Rouen. As to foreign designs appearing amidst thoroughly English work, as the examples in Devon at Coleridge, Colebrook and Brushford, all of the Brittany type, this may be accounted for from the fact that the lord of the manor, sir John Evans, spent much time in France under Henry VIII.

The work of the carpenters is of the greatest importance on the constructional side, erecting as they did a series of unrivalled timber roofs which remain one of the major glories of our country. The Brandons stated that:—

"In this feature of architecture England may be pronounced unrivalled; for though other countries may equal or excel her in the magnitude and external beauty of their churches, there is scarcely a church on the continent which can boast such timber roofs as are to be met with in almost every county of our land."

G. E. Street was even more enthusiastic, as was Francis Bond, and Viollet le Duc said "Si nous voulons voir les charpentes, il faut aller en Angleterre." Their construction included the arch-brace, the beam and the hammer, the last two brought to perfection in the fifteenth century. The noble panelled beam roofs of the clerestoried period, enriched with deep mouldings and decorated with carved bosses and crows' feet, is only matched by the double hammer-beams of East Anglia, a triumph of construction in which for once science and beauty are combined. These roofs harbour coveys of angels who perch upon every quoin of vantage and give the effect of a fluttering angelcote if one might be permitted to use such a term in regard to ethereal personages (153-4).

THE CRAFT OF THE GLAZIER

"In one sense at least art is a unity: it is the name we give to a certain human need—the need to see our perceptions and ideals externalised in appealing form; and this need is co-existent with the history of man."

HERBERT REED in *English Stained Glass*, page 1

THE art of colouring glass is one of considerable antiquity; it was practised as early as the fifth century, but the first mention of its use in England is in the year 680 when Benedict Biscop sent to Gaul for glaziers to come over and fill the windows of his two new stone foundations at Wearmouth and Jarrow. Twenty-five years later St. Wilfred followed his example for his new minister at York. These windows would consist of small pieces of coloured glass leaded together by "calmes" as this particular strip lead came to be called. Subject windows were not attempted before the tenth century, and it was as late as 1170 before they appeared in England, owing not only to their costliness but to the disturbed state of the country. These early windows were composed of small pieces of glass which had to be cut to shape by a grozing iron, which method was both tedious and extravagant in labour and time; the glass was thick and uneven in quality and deeply dyed; owing however to the impurity of the chemicals employed it was of uncertain tone, producing many variations and adding thereby considerably to the richness and sparkle of the windows.

There are remains of this twelfth-century glass at Canterbury (11), Dorchester, Oxon and York, the windows constructed of about fifty pieces to the square foot arranged principally in medallions which were placed in the aisles where they could be studied, and of single figures which were placed in the clerestories, these latter delineating the genealogy of Christ. The average figurework of this period is poorly drawn, badly proportioned especially so in hands and feet; nevertheless the figures are strongly visualised and grouped, forming a gorgeous mosaic of intense colour, principally ruby, blue, green, maroon, and pot metal. The large single round-headed windows were filled with many subjects arranged in large quatrefoils split up into a central square and four half-circles, also in diamonds and circles, each subject with an explanatory border in Lombardic lettering, the interstices filled with conventional scrolled

117 FRESSINGFIELD, SUFFOLK

116 WIGGENHALL, ST. M. VIRGIN
NORFOLK

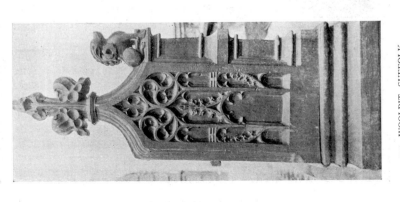

115 WOOLPIT, SUFFOLK

118 YORK MINSTER, CHAPTER· HOUSE

foliage, the window completed by a broad border. The backgrounds were simple in character with no attempt at perspective, indicating a building, a ship or castle, trees, waves, or if an interior a couch. Single figures often hold a scroll indicating their personality, and from the first the designers in various materials exchanged ideas, for the pose and setting of the figures representing virginity, continence, and marriage in the Canterbury window (11) bear a close resemblance to the arcade and figurework shown round the lead font at Ashover.

During the following period until about 1280 the earlier forms of medallions and single figures were continued, a little more accomplished in drawing but not quite so deeply stained. The flesh was no longer rendered in darkish brown but in a lighter brownish pink, the backgrounds remaining as before, either plain blue or ruby the borders becoming a little narrower. As this type of window prevented the admission of light owing to the depth of staining, a new type was evolved now known as grisaille, composed of a grey type of glass with a greenish tinge, designed in simple geometric patterning, the background being cross-hatched or otherwise filled in. The designs were quickly elaborated and a little coloured glass introduced, the patterns overlapping in rich profusion, the conventional foliage kept under control and confined to its own particular sections. Examples of grisaille are still at Salisbury, Lincoln (1) and elsewhere, the finest existing window however is in the north transept at York, consisting of five lights each 53 feet in height and 5 feet in width completely filled with grisaille. Interesting as it is to pick out the complicated geometric designs, it is apt to pall by constant repetition and by 1270 medallions were re-introduced to enliven the monotonous patterning, designed in circles, ovals, squares or quatrefoils as in the chapter-house at York (118). At the same time heraldry came into fashion, whose brilliant colours added greatly to the charm of the windows.

1280 to 1350. During this period glass reflects the advance and fashions made in other materials, and its increasing popularity helped the craftsmen to strike out with fresh ideas both in design and manipulation. The principal change apart from advancing technique and the use of larger pieces of glass lay in the discovery at the beginning of the fourteenth century of silver stain, which was eventually to change both the methods and face of painted glass, and to give to it a leading position among the crafts of the fifteenth century. Windows at this time were constructed of three or five lights and held far-reaching opportunities to the glaziers which the earlier single lights had

K

not vouchsafed to them; it led however to the temptation to ignore the mullions in designing the glass, which when it occurs is a sure sign of decadence. Window tracery was still beyond his control, he was therefore compelled to twist his figures and designs to fill the awkward shapes produced by the stonework which was in the hands of the mason, who designed the windows more for their own elegance than with any thoughts of what it would enclose. Another important advance in design was the canopy placed over a figure in a principal light; this is the complete answer to the framing and filling in of figure-work, and it has never been equalled. The canopies were first designed in a fairly simple style, with standards on either side of the figure, finishing in pinnacles and upholding an ogee arch, decorated with cusps and finial, shown at Deerhurst and York both in North St. and St. Denis. This however was soon elaborated, becoming a tall spire of tabernacle work, shown in the windows of the nave of York Minster, the Latin chapel of St. Frideswides, Oxford, the apse windows of Tewkesbury and in the great east window at Gloucester, where the spire is as elongated as the height of the figure it protects. These canopies were derived from the tombs and niches of the time and competed with the monumental brasses, whose origin came from the same source.

Grisaille was continued and quarries were either invented or utilised; the former now with a clear background, the cross-hatching disappearing. Toward the close of the thirteenth century foliage in glass was treated naturalistically, following the lead given by the stone carvers, the oak, vine, maple, and thorn all carefully drawn and often shown as starting from a central stem with spreading branches. Panels and heraldry were combined with grisaille with happy effect; later, single figures under short canopies were placed upon a quarry background as in the Latin chapel at Oxford. When connected foliage was not employed, the quarries had a separate decoration of flowers, stars, monograms, or butterflies as at St. Denis, York (120). The borders again become important decorative features, small blocks of plain colours alternating with heraldic badges and crests of royalty, patrons and donors, such as the triple-towered castle of Castille, the covered cup of Galacia, the lions and crowns at St. Denis, York, the *fleur-de-lys* at Credenhill, or lions heads and crowns with protruding tongues. When foliage was employed as the vine in the Oxford windows, the stems are often sprung from an animal or bird as the stork, the owl, or the ape (126); here again the belted ape is matched by a tile at Malmesbury (128), although in the glass the ape climbs, whereas

THIRTEENTH AND FOURTEENTH CENTURY GLASS, DONOR OFFERING HIS WINDOW. NOTICE QUARRIES AND BORDER

121 ST. FRIDESWIDE'S, OXFORD

120 ST. DENIS, YORK

119 TRYDDEN, N. WALES

122 YORK, HOLY TRINITY, GOODRAMGATE
CORONATION OF THE VIRGIN

123 MALVERN PRIORY. CHRIST AMONGST
THE DOCTORS

Sydney Pitcher, F.R.P.S. ph.

in the tile he takes the part of the doctor, the pose is the same in both.

The figures of this period have an exaggerated sway or poise, which may also be found in the sculptured figures of this time, and is vividly portrayed in the Annunciation subject in the Latin chapel at Oxford (121); the figures are tall and slim, their faces aloof and disinterested. The flesh tones continue a brownish pink, the garments however are gayly coloured. Saints now carry their emblems or have them placed in conjunction, the inscriptions continue the use of Lombardic lettering. The backgrounds of ruby, blue and green are no longer plain but enriched with intricate flowing foliage patterned upon them. Figures are sometimes placed upon a quarry background as at Eaton Bishop and Credenhill in Herefordshire, this is not always successful owing to the strong colours employed, such as the scarlet and green at Eaton Bishop where the value of the figure is diminished. Figures of donors appear for the first time, generally on the quarries below the panels as the donor offering his gift of the window at St. Denis, York (120). Tracery lights grow in importance in spite of their awkward shapes, single figures of saints appear in addition to grotesques, heraldry and foliage. Heraldry is used effectively, instead of a single coat of arms, the shields were now quartered, the ground-work of the shield diapered as in stone carving. Jesse trees owing to the size of the windows had now many figures and were much elaborated. Jesse laid at the base of the window and the Virgin occupying the top of the central light. At Dorchester priory the masons tried to compete, producing a Jesse window in stone, the glazier filling in the interspaces with additional figures. The general quality of the glass of this period was good, although still thick and uneven in texture, the white with a green cast, the other colours lovely and translucent especially the blues and greens as at Tewkesbury; the yellow of the silver satin became less brassy and as time went on more and more varied in tone.

With the approach of the fifteenth century, the work of the glazier had taken a strong hold on the imagination of the people, so much so that he was instrumental in helping to fashion the last great change in the architectural progression of the mediaeval period. We are apt to think that this change was brought about through the Black Death and the spread of the Severn style, or on account of the fifteenth century men's love of light; it would however be nearer the mark to suggest that it was his love of coloured glass. The exterior walls were turned into rows of four-light windows divided by heavy projecting buttresses, further additional windows added by building clerestories above the arcades. Furthermore the actual design of the stonework of the window was now due to the necessity of providing the glazier with panelled openings for his canopied figures. Indeed so complete was this domination of the glazier that in the great east windows now devoid of their original glass, Mr. Charles W. Baty asserts that it is possible in many instances to state the subject of the window by the arrangement of its tracery; this postulates that the tracery was designed for a given subject before it was erected, and that the donor and his glazier dictated its size and shape.

This popularity meant a large output of the glazier's art and there is every reason to suggest that shops sprang up in many parts of England, not only in the great cities but in the lesser towns. Naturally the quality of the work varied from the reputable firms such as Thornton and Prudde, to the small shop offering to fill a window in a country church at cut prices. It was also easier where the glazier had but little originality of his own to re-use his stock of shop cartoons by reversing them, altering small details, and counterchanging the colour scheme, and this was often the case. Mr. Knowles has pointed out instances in the glass at York not only in the Minster but elsewhere. These many centres had their own individualities of style, though at the present time we have much to learn as to the provenance of the differences noted. We know something of the glass produced in the London shops and those of York and Coventry, but are uncertain of others. Unfortunately few centres have left any record or remains on which to build up a careful analysis of details of drawing and mannerisms of style. The forerunner of the fifteenth century style both as regards glass and stonework is found in the extraordinary east window of the quire at Gloucester, which according to the arms therein portrayed has been dated as early as 1350, at least forty years before its time. It remains also the largest window of its class being 78 feet in height and 38 feet in width. Not only in its stonework but in its glass it is thoroughly fifteenth century; the panels are filled with single figures originally facing each other in pairs, the backgrounds of ruby and blue counterchanged. The figures were made from white glass, the garments with stained borders, the haloes of coloured glass. The subject of the entire window is the Coronation of the Virgin by her Son, attended by the hierarchy including the founders and ecclesiastical dignitaries of Gloucester abbey.

The architectural style of the fifteenth century was a return to stability, from the flowing to the vertical, from the flamboyant to the structurally sound; the glass of the period was also architectural in feeling, composed largely of single figures under canopies, or subject panels, generally square in shape set in rows, each under its low canopy. There is a spirit of refinement and finish in the drawing, a careful study of personality in the figures, and a sense of culture lacking in the earlier styles. The shading is stippled instead of smeared, with more gradations and a warmer tone. The colouring is softer and less intense but sparklingly clear, there is a larger proportion of white glass treated with silver stain, the properties and advantages of which were fully appreciated and used; indeed many windows were wholly made in this way with a minimum of colour added. The figures are taller and more graceful in poise, the garments looser in the folds and richly shaded. Features are carefully drawn, the eyes correctly delineated and many of the faces are truly beautiful and full of character.

There was a change in inscriptions to black letter about 1380, these were shortened and in monks' Latin, more difficult to decipher than the earlier Lombardic. Many figures carry scrolls or have scrolls of a wavy character about them; if apostles with sentences of the Creed, if prophets, quotations from the old Testament, bits of the *Te Deum* or the name of the person represented. Figures stand upon bases which like the canopies above are now three dimensional, drawn in perspective. The canopies are shorter and fuller with plenty of invention in the drawing and detail; they are mostly in white glass with coloured backgrounds, and have many quaint conceits, in Yorkshire little angels hop about the pinnacles and niches. The backgrounds behind the principal figures are enriched with seaweedy patterns in place of the earlier scrollwork. The tracery heads of the windows are filled with small figures of saints or angels, if the latter, either members of the inner orders, or bearing shields of arms, singing or playing instruments. On occasion the tracery lights seem to have been the work of apprentices; they are rarely as carefully done as the main lights, the iris is often omitted and the drapery stiff and square in its folds. The angels are clothed in albs or wear feathered tights as in the mystery plays from which so many costumes and scenes were taken by the craftsmen of the middle ages.

During this time subject pictures were popular, the east window of York Minster which contains 1,700 square feet of glass has over 120 subject panels. Windows were designed either with single figures or subject panels depicting the lives of the Virgin (125), Christ and the saints. There is much variety in treatment, the Crucifixion was drawn with simplicity and dignity and often formed the reredos to the altar; the Trinity was also popular. Jesse windows continued to be made but were not as numerous as before. Donors were shown together with their families, placed in the bottom corners of the window, the husband and his boys in one panel (124), the wife and girls in the opposite panel. Heraldry was increasingly used and was placed in almost any position, even in the canopy as at Almondbury, Yorks (127). The Wars of the Roses seem to have had little effect upon either output or quality, for it was not so much a civil war as a squabble of the aristocracy. The period reached its highest point about 1485, after which date there was a slow but perceptible decline; by 1490 the shading had become heavy and opaque, and the trend to pictorialism was gaining ground, helped by the men of Flanders who were invited by the king to work in this country, and whose idea seemed to be to rival the painter at his job, abandoning the restraint imposed upon him by the architectural setting to his work. The mullions and tracery instead of framing the glaziers designs were now an obstacle to his conceptions and cut across his picture in an arbitrary way, shown at Fairford in the Crucifixion window, where a horse is cut in two. The true function of painted glass quickly disappeared, and was helped by the discovery of enamelling different colours onto a large sheet of glass. This has never proved a satisfactory method, the enamelled colours having a tendency to flake off. Leading also lost touch with design and no longer bore any relation to the subject. The attempt to copy the work of the painters in the natural treatment of figures and landscape, and to rival them in glass was a disaster, the heavy shading and complicated grouping tended to a loss of transparency and sparkle. In the earlier examples the setting was observed, as the two Jesse windows at Thornhill in Yorkshire and Llanrhaiadr in Denbigh, but the work of the foreign craftsmen ignored this, as can be seen in the windows of King's College chapel at Cambridge and at Fairford where the Crucifixion window exhibits a restless fussiness, a lack of dignity, and a pictorial aspect totally alien to the finest traditions of the English craft.

125 ALMONDBURY, YORKSHIRE, ANNE TEACHING
THE VIRGIN TO READ

124 BOWNESS, WESTMORLAND, TWO DONORS. FORMERLY
AT CARTMEL PRIORY

128 MALMESBURY ABBEY

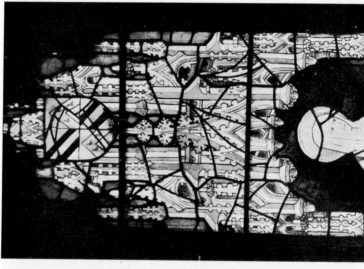

127 ALMONDBURY, YORKS

126 OXFORD, ST. FRITESWIDE'S

PAINTED DECORATION

"The spirit of the time is perhaps best studied in the North; for here rather than in the South, we find the source of that vitality, intensely idealistic yet human and gay, which is the key-note of the Gothic spirit."

Prof. E. W. TRISTRAM, *Archaeologia*, Vol. 76, page 184

THE question of the earlier art of painting, either in the form of illuminated manuscripts or of wall paintings, can be the better understood with the knowledge that it formed but a part of the magnificent output of the mediaeval period, which included embroidery, stained glass, ivory and alabaster carving, and figurework in stone, marble, wood, metal and enamels, all correlated not only in artistic aims and format, but in the doctrinal teaching which it was intended to convey. Although the bold outlines of the drawing, the pose of the figure and the subjects portrayed altered from one phase to another, they are faithfully reflected in each differing medium in turn, all having a common origin and source; the craftsman adapting his material to his needs in such a manner that the subject delineated often brought out its particular qualities, giving that touch of naïve inspiration which marked it out from amongst the general mass production of the fraternities and shop gilds.

The sources of our somewhat scanty knowledge of the earliest paintings executed in Britain are twofold; that in which we have to rely upon references to be found in the writings of the early historians, the other in the admirable illuminated manuscripts which have survived, and are unfortunately outside our scope. The former includes a statement that in A.D. 674 Bishop Wilfred caused the walls of his new cathedral at York to be painted. Although perhaps examples survive of paintings executed in the eleventh century, it is not until the twelfth that we can actually put a date to our English paintings. At this time the country was recovering from the effects of the Invasion, and from then until the suppression paintings continued to be produced in ever-increasing numbers, after which date they were either destroyed or obliterated by whitewash. So thoroughly was this accomplished that in the large majority of cases we owe our knowledge to the recoveries made from defaced or obliterated paintings found upon walls, vaults, tombs, and furniture, and also in the building accounts connected with Westminster abbey, in which several names therein recorded gradually become personalities, such as William formerly of Winchester and now of Westminster called "the king's beloved painter" 1240; Thomas of Durham 1261, and his son Richard, and later, Master Hugh of St. Albans.

At Canterbury cathedral in the chapel of St. Anselm is a nearly perfect example of early twelfth century painting. It owes its preservation in that it was walled up shortly after its execution, and so remained to within recent years. The subject is St. Paul at Melita bitten by a viper, a figure both dignified and noble. The draperies suggest those delineated in manuscripts, and are similar to the apostles in the lunettes of the south porch at Malmesbury (48). There are other interesting remains of early painting in the crypt chapel of St. Gabriel in the same cathedral. At Kempley, Gloucestershire, the chancel shows a fairly complete scheme of decoration, the side walls have a series of apostles under a continuous arcade, the figures not only dignified but thoroughly decorative in character. These should be compared with the window at Canterbury depicting virginity, continence, and marriage (11), and the decoration applied to the circular fonts in stone and lead of the period (58, 189–191). Other remains of this time are to be found at Chaldon, Chalgrove and Hardham; at Copford the scheme though much restored is complete both on the apse and chancel arch. The former has a Majesty with angels and a series of apostles below. The Hardham series includes the Fall, and scenes from the life and Passion of our Lord including the torments in hell. The Barfreston paintings have been destroyed. At Durham in the Lady chapel are fragments of a decorative scheme of some importance, showing remarkable perceptions as to the values of purely arbitrary design. Another vast piece of decoration is the nave roof of Peterborough cathedral which may be dated about 1220. Although it has been repainted it retains its original setting out. It is designed as a series of inter-locking lozenges or diamond-shaped panels; these consist of twelfth century border patterns, the centre of many of the diamonds containing the figures of kings, bishops, saints, angels playing musical instruments and fabulous animals. The inner spaces measure 90 inches by 42 although from below they appear quite tiny.

During the thirteenth century England was well known for the excellence of its painting, embroidery, tiles and stained glass, although unfortunately we have little to show of the period. The painting had the same quality as the sculpture, the figures were attenuated, aloof, full of nobility and grace; this is illustrated by the figure of St. Faith in the chapel of that

130 LUDHAM, NORFOLK, SCREEN PANELS

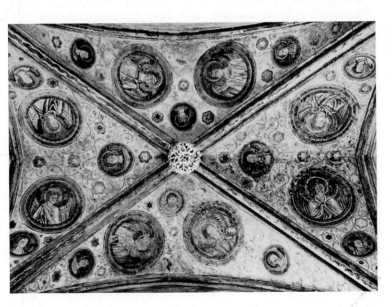

129 WINCHESTER CATHEDRAL, VAULT OF THE CHAPEL
OF THE GUARDIAN ANGELS

131 RANWORTH, NORFOLK, SCREEN PANEL

name at Westminster abbey, the work no doubt of the king's beloved painter William of Winchester. Below the saint is a predella of the Crucifixion with Mary and John, the treatment is entirely removed from realism and both in the drawing and the pose of the figures the subject is etherealised. Of about the same date is perhaps the loveliest bit of mediaeval painting we possess, namely the Virgin and Child from the bishop's chapel at Chichester (132); a quatrefoil within a circle, a portion of a larger scheme. The exquisite and tender feeling here expressed both in the drawing and pose is supplemented by the delicacy of the colouring.

Master Walter of Colchester became a monk at St. Albans earlier in the century, and is described by a brother monk Matthew Paris as that incomparable painter; his brother Simon and his son Richard also worked there and it is recorded that they produced seven reredoses. Perhaps the earliest existing painting on the nave piers may have been by him, the later ones are not so good. Of the earlier painting of this century those at Winchester in the chapel of the Holy Sepulchre have a vitality and power extraordinary even when compared with contemporary work. Other paintings are at Clayton and Patcham in Sussex and elsewhere. Again at Winchester 1250–60 painted upon the vault of the chapel of the Guardian Angels, are medallions (129) containing demi-angels, the ground between interspersed with foliage and flowers. The mangled remains of a splendid work (1260) is the retable at Westminster which originally consisted of five panels decorated with gold, glass and enamels in addition to the painting of single figures and subject panels, and when perfect must indeed have presented a glorious scheme of colour.

With the turn of the century we reach perhaps the highest point in mediaeval painting in which a gay idealism, combined with drawing in bold outline and primitive colouring, was as yet unspoilt by realism and a greater knowledge of technique which gradually developed into professionalism. In Westminster abbey are the remains of several attractive works of the early part of the fourteenth century. The Coronation chair 1300 is the work of Master Walter, the king's painter to Edward I. It was covered over with flat gesso the whole coloured and gilt. On the north side of the quire are three canopied tombs to Edmund Crouchback, his wife Aveline and Aymer de Valence earl of Pembroke; when first erected they were a blaze of gold and colours, with glass mosaics now vanished. The canopies, tombs, effigies and weepers all received their share of enrichment; on the sub-base of the Crouchback tomb on the north side was painted a series of ten knights in lively attitudes carrying banners, limned in natural pose and shown with the sway peculiar to the period. On the opposite side of the quire stands the wooden sedilia once richly decorated, and still retaining two panelled figures within, and the lower half of an Annunciation without. The interior figures are those of Henry III and Edward I standing over eight feet in height and drawn with a rhythmical pose of figure and drapery. Perhaps the finest series of wall paintings of this date is to be found at Croughton, Northants. They are superior to the average wall paintings found hidden under the whitewash, for there is a certainty of touch, a sense of composition, a dignity and grace which combine to make them one of the finest achievements of English work; for their origin we must I think look to the East Anglian school of illuminators. The subjects illustrate incidents in the lives of our Lord and the Blessed Virgin, the scenes are picked out in red, yellow and blue upon an ivory ground, the treatment varying from the simple to the dramatic. Other churches having wall paintings of this time are Chalgrove, Oxon. and Hailes in Gloucestershire. The former paintings are designed in three tiers and illustrate incidents in the life of the Virgin; at Hailes the treatment is unusual, showing large spaces of diapering composed of heraldic devices, whilst above is a series of single figures placed under an arcade. In the chapter-house at Westminster are painted panels of the late fourteenth century date and in the presbytery an extraordinary easel portrait of Richard II, perhaps the finest existing portrait of its date (1390) to be found in the whole of Europe. Lethaby suggests Herebrecht of Cologne as the painter, for he was engaged upon work for St. Paul's in London; however Messrs. Borenius and Tristram suggest an English origin.

During the latter part of this century the painting of religious subjects was supplemented by folk-lore and certain legends of more or less secular origin, one of great popularity being that of Piers Plowman in which Christ is represented as Piers surrounded by the everyday tools of the labourer and artisan, a concession made by the church to a popular demand. The poem was written amongst the Malvern hills and made a strong and urgent democratic appeal to a feudal world as yet largely untouched by the needs of the populace. In the fifteenth century the scope of subject was further enlarged and included moralities, historical scenes and incidents from the lives of the saints. Such moralities as "The Quick and the Dead," "The Seven Acts of Mercy," "The Seven Deadly Sins," and the Doom appealed strongly, as did scenes from the lives of certain

132. THE VIRGIN AND CHILD, WALL PAINTING, *ca.* 1260, IN THE
CHAPEL OF THE BISHOP'S PALACE, CHICHESTER

saints especially their martyrdoms and horrid ends. Saints Christopher, Katherine, Martin and Nicholas became intermediaries for the common people. The Last Judgment with Michael weighing the souls and the wicked being pitchforked into the mouth of hell by grinning devils who enjoyed every minute of the time was placed above the Rood screen for all to see. When it is remembered that the services were in an unknown tongue and, that after the Black Death the average priest was none too learned, the importance of painting the walls and windows with scenes for the purpose of inculcating doctrine cannot be exaggerated. Each saint held a special office. St. Christopher was the protector from sudden death and for those taking a journey. He was therefore painted on the wall opposite the main entrance to the church carrying the Child Christ upon his shoulder, wading across a river with a lantern in one hand and the staff that blossomed in the other, so that everyone passing the doorway could glance in and be protected during that day. It is quite evident that the church tolerated and gave way to popular appeal regarding apocryphal incidents in the lives of the saints, and cast an indulgent eye upon the accumulation of curious detail, often of a macabre character which became attached to the original legend, and which the people delighted to have set before them. Local saints and their doings, dragons and monsters dire, martyrdoms especially the gruesome ones such as that of St. Erasmus who was disembowelled by having his intestines wound round a windlass. The people had a childlike love of beauty and a fascination for horrors, they in fact loved to be thrilled exactly as do the constant attenders of the cinema of today.

In painting, the fifteenth century showed a great advance in technique and accomplishment, so much so that a large percentage of the work may be classed as professional or shopwork in its origin. This however had and still has a very considerable drawback, for it is a truism that the greater the technique the less the inspiration; we have only to compare the amateur thirteenth century rendering of the Virgin and Child in the bishop's chapel at Chichester with the professional painting of the saints on the panels of the screen at Cawston, Norfolk, to realise what an irreparable loss has been sustained in the process; we have already noticed the same deterioration taking place in other mediums such as the statuary of the shop-gild period, tomb design, and metalwork, and in the later sixteenth century in stained glass and heraldry. Wall paintings were continued as at Pickering and Friskney, but we know the period better by the output of paintings upon wooden panels, either reredoses or in the decoration of screens and the like. The notable reredos preserved in Norwich cathedral owes its continued existence to the fact that the underside of it was used as a table. It illustrates the Passion of Christ and may be dated about 1400. The colouring is lovely and delicate, but in general treatment it is a little sophisticated (133). Here as elsewhere the backgrounds have a patterned relief in gold. Other panels remain in the church of St. Michael-at-Plea, Norwich, and several are preserved in museums now divorced from their proper surroundings and losing half their effect.

The erection of numberless wooden screens during this century provided the opportunity for painting many series of saints upon the lower panelling, which was divided into narrow spaces surmounted by traceried heads. Large numbers survive both in East Anglia and the South-west, the former the more accomplished, the latter the more vigorous if crude. Many of the Anglian paintings show distinct continental influence, but not all. Perhaps Ranworth might be selected as an example of unusual excellence (131), the faces are delicately drawn, the figures well proportioned and supremely decorative, while their golden robes are diapered with the finest damask patterning. The nine orders of angels on blue grounds in the north aisle screen at Southwold are even more decorative. Their golden wings, lovely garments decorated with jewels, bells and pomegranates are wonderfully effective, and the faces are refined and beautiful. Barton Turf is almost as good, together with St. Michael-at-Plea, Norwich. At Loddon there are scenes containing several figures drawn in strong outline as in wall paintings. In Devonshire the more artless figures are still attractive and Bradninch, Ashton and Plymtree may be noted. Dooms, once plentiful, painted upon the tympanums above the screens, have been cast out during nineteenth century restorations, but one or two remain in a mutilated condition at Southleigh, Oxon, Wenhaston Suffolk now in the body of the church, and elsewhere.

At Eton college chapel a series of wall paintings were discovered in 1923 dating from about 1480, and illustrating incidents connected with the life of the Virgin. The square panels alternate with niched single figures of saints. The figures are almost life-size and are painted largely in monochrome with touches of colour. They are perhaps the most important examples of the painters' art of the period, lively in pose and full of character; they partake however of the quality of easel paintings and show a close approach to the Renaissance work of the sixteenth and seventeenth centuries.

It is perhaps not sufficiently realised to what an extent coloured decoration was employed from quite early times. Norman doorways and arches which are now plain and commonplace were originally painted with the same patterning with which the more important door-heads and arches were carved, and these carved mouldings were nevertheless painted in various colours. The same applies to the pier-caps, in fact to any place where suitable decoration could be placed; the great cylindrical piers were patterned in chevrons, diamonds, reeds, and spirals, as are shown incised at Durham, Lindisfarne, Waltham and elsewhere. These Norman moulding patterns were used as borderings as late as 1300, as at Croughton, Northants.

Throughout the whole mediaeval period the decorating of walls, roofs, vaults, window jambs, furniture in wood and stone and tombs was continued with the additional help of gesso, glass mosaic and enamelling. The walls of churches were generally whitened to something of the colour of parchment, and upon this was a decoration of vermilion and gold arranged in lines like masonry and each space sprigged with a rose. At Westminster this decoration was continued in the cloister with the addition of wall paintings, legends and gilding. The vaulting generally received adornment, as in Westminster cloister and Ely, where in 1336 the rebuilt vault of the quire was decorated by Master William Shank, the scheme principally confined to the vaulting ribs and bosses. These were covered with vermilion and gold, a large quantity of the latter being employed. There is a note in the Sacrist's Roll for that year paying Radulphus le Gold-beter for making gold-leaf for Master Shank from the Prior's florins. At Exeter in 1316–17 during the erection of the reredos, sedilia and pulpitum, Nicholas the painter and figure sculptor received 2s. a week, lesser painters, Leva, Boteler, and Berested, eighteen pence and less, and Richard the colour grinder was paid twelve pence. A marble stone was found on which to grind the colours and twelve discs for rubbing the colours to powder, together with woven linen for straining the colours.

The mediaeval system was to use each colour in its purest and brightest form, avoiding large expanses, and working on heraldic rules. Counterchange was in constant use and in mouldings each colour was separated by a line of white. This coloured decoration was applied equally to wood or stone, the carving generally gilt with red shadows. We may conclude our remarks by a quotation from the late W. R. Lethaby in his book *Westminster Abbey re-examined:*—

"The tombs of the interior, lately cleaned, show what the painted sculpture was like. The knights and ladies had bright eyes, flushed cheeks, and coloured garments. The effigy of the Lady Aveline was painted all over; she had a red robe and green mantle lined with blue. The pillow was diapered with coats of arms, which were painted in transparent varnish colours over gold. Crouchback's effigy had a red surcoat diapered with a pattern imitated from the retable; on the front of it was a big coat of arms. The flesh was painted, the cheeks flushed, and the eyes had blue circles. The little angels at his head were fully coloured and their hair gilt.

"The weepers had red cheeks and painted garments—in some cases, at least, these seem to have been in varnish colour over gold. The ornamental painting of these two tombs was so elaborate that no description would serve without illustrations. Little panels were inlaid with glass over patternwork on gold, other parts were in raised gesso gilt, even the little knight in the gable of Crouchback's tomb had red cheeks, and he rode a dappled horse."

133. THE FLAGELLATION, PANEL FROM A RETABLE
IN NORWICH CATHEDRAL

LIFE, NATURAL AND SUPERNATURAL DEPICTED BY THE MEDIAEVAL CARVERS

"Bewar of the devyl when he blawis his horn."
from Campsall screen, Yorks

FROM a study of the lesser carvings from the twelfth century onwards, the conclusion is gradually pressed home that these early craftsmen were possessed not only of a lively imagination but a sense of grim humour, shown not only in their treatment of angels, devils and humanity, but also in a world of phantasy, whose origin, though coming through classical sources, was steeped in the amalgam of the mediaeval mind and transfused into creatures whose habits and histories, however far-fetched, were used to point a moral; macabre two-headed monsters and combinations of animals and birds whose questionable lives behoved one to give them a wide berth. These rather horrible writhing deformities belong to the earlier time, where they are represented as torturing the sinners either by biting out their eyes or tongues, or leech-like, sucking away their life-blood, shown on a loose capital in the museum at York (136), and on a corbel in the north transept at Bottesford. Dragons, wyverns, centaurs, harpies, monkeys, crocodiles (134) and horned bestialities abound, decorating capitals, doorheads, corbels, and, as at Studham, Beds, where encircling the font, are particularly loathsome amphisbaena. Many twelfth-century doorways are studded with hideous masks and faces, the result of an unrestrained imagination or an uncultivated mind worthy of the Nazi sadistic outlook; the majority however were carved to teach and enforce the doctrines of the church and inculcate the consequences of disobedience.

How much of this was believed or was symbolical we do not know, but St. Bernard in his denunciation of luxury says that in the cloisters it was possible to see "one head with many bodies, or one body with many heads. Here is a quadruped with a serpent's tail; there a fish with a beast's head; there a centaur, in front a horse, behind a goat; another has horns at one end, and a horse's tail at another." He further speaks of the monks admiring these oddities, and finishes "Good God! if we are not ashamed of these absurdities, why do we not grieve at the cost of them?" so that it would appear that in his time these carvings were considered conceits. This early ascetic attitude of the soul fighting the world and its iniquities in addition to that of the devil with his enormities gave place in the fourteenth century to a brighter outlook and an easier mind. The fiend and all his works assumed much less importance and the world became a pleasanter spot at least for the favoured few. The monstrous and the macabre disappearerd from the points of vantage and were relegated to the carvings under the seats of the stallwork, where may be found every conceivable oddity, culled from the early books on natural history called Bestiaries, such as the one written about 1210-11 by Guillaume le Clerc. These tomes are crammed with stories and drawings of mandrakes, cockatrice, corpse-eating hyenas, caladrius, worms with heads at either end, hydras and gorgons dire; a gallery of nightmare curiosities of the greatest interest for those in search of wonders.

In the earlier period the devil was allowed a certain majesty as he superintended the pitchforking of the souls of the damned into the mouth of hell; unfortunately the majority of Dooms have perished. There is an early sculptured example in the cathedral library at York and a thirteenth-century one in the eastern wall arcading at Worcester, where the torments of the sinners are realistically depicted, and a richly coloured design in glass at Fairford as well as a fragmentary one at York. The devil is often represented with eagles' legs and crowned with horns. By the fifteenth century however his brood became the subject of satire, descending to pot-house revels; they are shown humorously pinched in the stonework in the Southwell pulpitum and the Beverley reredos; they wander about at Lincoln and Chester, and are to be found lurking in the foliage near an angel in the Harrington tomb at Cartmel, and peeping out of a spandrel of a tomb at Tewkesbury and from other canopies. Their later escapades were principally outside the church, scrambling amongst the gargoyles and parapets (138), helping contorted creatures to spew out the rainwater and in other ways resembling more the sprite than the spirit of evil, and carved with a cynical sense of humour. The devil is the butt of many a crude joke, his authority seemingly could be flouted in public, even when his power was felt in private; later he becomes the clown of the mediaeval stage, and his direct descendant is Punch whose antics it is still our privilege to enjoy occasionally.

Angels were represented in carving from quite early times and are found on the font at Lenton, the doorway at Kilpeck (137) and the chancel arch at Rowlestone; they gradually enjoyed a popularity which continued for the whole of the

136　YORK MUSEUM, MONSTER
137　KILPECK, EARLY ANGEL

134　KILPECK, CROCODILE HEAD. HEREFORDSHIRE
135　ELKSTONE, GLOUCESTERSHIRE, VAULTING BOSS

138 WINDSOR, ST. GEORGE, EXTERIOR GARGOYLE
139 HEDON, YORKSHIRE, TERMINATION OF STRING COURSE
140 EXETER CATHEDRAL, MERMAID HOLDING A FISH
141 EXETER CATHEDRAL, CATERPILLARS IN THE FOLIAGE
142 YORK CHAPTER-HOUSE, MONKEY WHIPPING ITS YOUNG
143 RIPON CATHEDRAL, ELEPHANT WITH ITS HOWDAH

mediaeval period. They are far away the most important of the supernatural powers and formed a comprehensive army known as the Hierarchy of angels which was divided into nine orders. The first three, Cherubim, Seraphim, and Thrones were placed immediately round the throne of God to worship him and sing his praise. In the fifteenth century they were represented as feathered creatures with bare hands and feet, standing upon flames, each having three pairs of wings; they hold their hands on high proclaiming the majesty of God. The second order of the three comprise Dominations, Virtues, and Powers; these govern the universality of people in common, Dominations with two pairs of wings have robes over their feathers and carry books, standing upon clouds. Virtues hold many differing emblems in their hands but are otherwise similar to their companions. Powers hold the sword and sceptre of state and trample upon dragons, devils and evil generally. The last series of three embrace Principalities, Archangels and angels; the first are clothed as are Powers bearing almost the same emblems; Archangels have each two pairs of wings and hold their appropriate symbols, St. Michael with a spear and shield; St. Gabriel with a sheaf of lilies. The employment of the ordinary angel was to be the servant of all, waiting upon and censing the paths of the saints as at Warwick (67), forming heavenly orchestras and choirs; there is a complete orchestra over the great altar in the quire at Gloucester (55), on the minstrels' gallery at Exeter and on Bp. Branscombe's tomb canopy at the same place; also the angel quire at Lincoln and the Percy tomb at Beverley. On a tomb at St. Katherine's Hospital, London, the angels blow silver trumpets, while in the enrichment above, others support the arms of the duke. They also appear in the fine timber roofs at Manchester and did in St. Mary's hall, Coventry (156). They hold the emblems of the Lord's Passion at Gresford and many other places.

Complete Hierarchies of angels may be seen in glass at New College, Oxford and St. Neots, Cornwall, with a charming series sculptured on the east wall of the Beauchamp chapel at Warwick (67, 146, 155). Mediaeval angels are represented as males and their costumes were taken in the fifteenth century from the Mystery plays, in which they were shown in coloured and gilt feathered tights, with bare hands and feet; they are on a totally different plane to the insipid, sentimental sugary female angels which have now become inhabitants of our churches; it would be instructive to know the date and reason for this change of sex.

The ordinary angel however was given other occupations, for

M

he was requisitioned to work upon earth for the honour of knights and their ladies, carefully carrying their souls to heaven in a winding sheet, as sculptured on the tombs at Beverley, Cartmel, Bainton and Long Wittenham, guarding the pillows of the ladies as at Ewelme, more often standing in rows as the servants of the squire, holding his shields quartered with his arms and those of his wife and ancestors. So secular did their labours become with consorting with human beings, that they are to be found hawking and hunting on the shrine of St. William at York and in the angel quire at Lincoln. They are carved holding ribbons upon which inscriptions were painted, as in the chancel at Hillesden; others form the enrichment to mouldings and are often crowded together with shields, emblems or ribbonwork as at Windsor, Westminster, Winchester, Hitchin (168), and on monuments at Long Ashton and St. Mary Redcliffe.

The angel's wing formed a happy decorative feature for the filling of spandrels, and was so used at Westminster (66), where also the swinging censer fulfils the same purpose; these angels in the transept triforiums have never been surpassed in dignity, beauty and grace, and are the high water-mark of decorative sculpture. The London school continued to produce lovely angels, especially the set at Warwick on the east wall of the Beauchamp chapel. Although diminutive in size, much thought was expended upon them and the angels of the Nativity, Expulsion (146) and Gabriel are extraordinarily beautiful. If these are a sample of what we have lost elsewhere it has indeed been grievous. Angels are not all alike; they have as much individuality as the districts from which they emanate. In the south-west they have a bird-like quality, and are delightful little creatures nestling by the pillows of the deceased, as at Long Ashton and Colyton; otherwise their wings are brought straight above their heads, each feather growing away from the next, as at St. Mary Redcliffe and Sugar's chantry chapel at Wells. The York type of the fourteenth century is robust, a little florid with wavy hair, a little self-confident, which is possibly a characteristic of that county. The ethereal angel of the Annunciation, now on a pedestal at Howden (53), is dignified and shows the York school at its best. The alabaster centres had their own type, sedate and impersonal from Chelleston, and with swallow-like wings from Nottingham. The woodworkers had taken angels to their hearts, and innumerable roofs were and are still adorned and crowded with them, either pinned on or actually cut out of the hammer-beams; they hold emblems, shields, musical instruments or lift up their hands in praise (153-4);

146 WARWICK, BEAUCHAMP CHANTRY, ANGEL OF THE EXPULSION

145 BARFREYSTONE DOORWAY, FOX PLAYING HARP

144 ST. MARY, BEVERLEY HARE GOING HUNTING

147 SALISBURY, CHAPTER-HOUSE, AND 148, 149 TIVERTON, GREENWAY CHAPEL

when coloured and gilt they must have been a glorious and imposing sight. The wooden figures over the Suffolk tomb at Ewelme are possibly of London origin, and give us a glimpse of the woodworkers' mastery of the figure.

The baberies or carving on the brackets under the seats of the stallwork, together with the subjects illustrated on elbow rests, popeys, and parochial benching, form a splendid contribution to our knowledge of the life and thought of the craftsmen of the middle ages. The subjects carved cover a wide field, and it is apparent that the carver was little hampered in his choice of subject, hardly ever working to a set scheme, but generally from personal choice. Many subjects are common to several sets, others individual to a locality or time; nevertheless there are unmistakable signs in the last period that the craftsmen copied illustrations which were in circulation, for not only are the details of certain subjects alike but the position in which the figures are placed is the same; these copies are not all by the same men, judging from the technique and cutting.

The earlier the set the more monsters it contains, as at Chichester; in the early fourteenth century, however, delightful nature studies were carved at Wells; later, about 1380 the technique of the craftsmen employed at Chester is bordering on the marvellous in its minuteness and care for detail. The subjects illustrated embrace, in addition to mythical beasts, religious subjects and incidents in the lives of the saints; the seasons are depicted; there are illustrations from the romances of the time and cunning fables in which animals take the part of human beings (144). There are domestic scenes of a homely character, and sport and pastimes come under review, nature studies, coats-of-arms, rebusues, inscriptions, architectural detail, and, in addition to all this a sarcastic and cynical view of the faithfulness of monks and nuns to their vows as of the tempers of married women, shown in domestic infelicities; in fact little escaped the vigilant eyes of the craftsmen as they made their mental notes for future use. It is more than evident that they enjoyed their work and the freedom it gave them from enforced design; it was not only a relief but a mental holiday.

Certain subjects cover a wide field of area and popularity, the writer has noted twenty-one carvings of mermen and maids emanating from every district, not only on baberies but roof bosses as at Exeter (140). The same may be said of the elephant, with or without his howdah, the craftsmen preferring the imaginative drawing in the Bestiaries to the real animal. There is a fine carving on a popey head of a stall-end at Ripon (143), another at Willian, Herts. He is found at Ottery St. Mary on a capital, and was used as the city arms of Coventry, where he was carved in the roof of St. Mary's hall and on the chair of the mayor. Studies of the cat and mouse go back to the thirteenth century and are found at Winchester, Wells, and on pier-caps in the chapter-houses at Lichfield and York, also at Beverley and New College, Oxford. At Malvern the rats are busily engaged in hanging the cat on a gibbet, and at Wells she plays the fiddle (1280–1320) our nursery rhymes going well back into the past. The Wells baberies were carved at the short time during which the craftsmen were transcribing nature, and they show a succession of lifelike studies of dogs, cats, rabbits, hares, bats, sheep, peacocks and eagles as well as budgerigars; at Winchester college chapel a shepherd carries two lambs in his arms. There are cocks, hens and chickens at Beverley, Tewkesbury, and Wells. A lizard is found on a corbel at Wells wriggling through the trefoil leaves, at Ely in the Alcock chantry there are brackets composed of snails and their shells, while at Bristol in the vestibule to the Berkeley chapel the weather moulding of the doorway is carved with ammonites, their shells forming the design.

Birds are used as decoration; they form the cusps to a screen at Burgh, Lincs, as the crestings of a screen at Exeter and to Bird's chantry chapel at Bath. They were prominent in the bosses of St. Mary's hall, Coventry, fighting dragons and other beasts. At Hawton in the sedilia the Pelican in her Piety much resembles a cockatoo, as does the lectern at St. Cross Hospital. The owl teased by birds is found in many places, the finest at Norwich. The Holy Ghost in the form of a bird is crowned at Stratford by two other birds. The pig is a prime favourite, with lord and husbandman, monk and clergy. As the tythe pig she is carved on a boss at Ugborough, Devon and the porch of St. Cuthbert's Wells. At Llanrwst a tracery head of the screen is designed as an oak tree wherein the pigs disport themselves. At Beverley on a reredos boss the herdsmen knock down the acorns for the pigs below, whilst birds sing in the branches. At Manchester the sow plays a harp, at Ripon bagpipes, where the little piglets dance to the music. At Exeter the caterpillars eat the foliage of a boss (141), and in another the squirrels crack the nuts of the filbert tree of which it is composed.

Windmills are shown at Bristol and on a bench at Bishops Lydiard (150). The parapets of the Greenway chapel at Tiverton are enriched with ships of a thrilling nature (148–9), which are supplemented by others on the bench-ends at East Budleigh (152) and Bps. Lydiard; at St. Davids are two baberies of ship

152 EAST BUDLEIGH

151 EAST BRENT

150 BISHOP LYDIARD

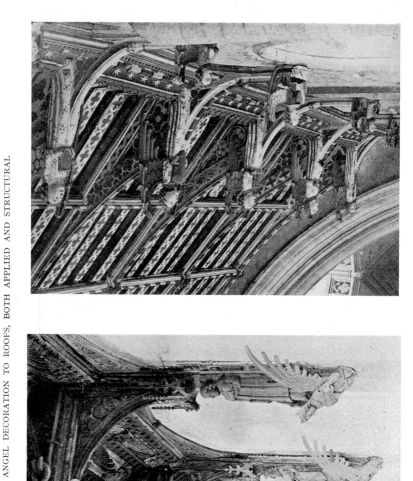

156.—COVENTRY, ST. MARY GILDHALL, NOW DESTROYED

155 WARWICK, BEAUCHAMP CHAPEL

157 COVENTRY, ST. MICHAEL, "THE STEM OF JESSE," DESTROYED BY NAZIS
158 WHALLEY, LANCASHIRE, "SHOEING THE GOOSE"
159 WORCESTER CATHEDRAL, "THE TOURNAMENT"

building and tarring the seams; on the second the voyage has started and one of the crew is violently sick. Everyday life and agriculture are found in the sets of the seasons at Malvern, Ripple and Lincoln, as elsewhere including the slaughtering of the pig. Sport and pastimes have a prominent place, bear-baiting at Beverley, Bristol, Manchester and St. Germains, also on the enrichment of the watching chamber at St. Albans. Hawking and hunting the stag, boar and hare with dogs are common, and for indoor games chequers and backgammon are played; on a capital at Winchester a man is carved carrying a chequer-board; at Manchester two men are seated playing backgammon. There are representations of tumblers, acrobats and itinerant musicians as well as clowns. Schooling is depicted by a boy laid across his master's knee, his breeches turned down receiving corporal punishment to the delight of the other scholars; there are good examples of this punishment at Sherborne, Boston and Norwich. Wrestling matches generally between man and man, but sometimes between man and bear or lion, knights in their armour returning from the wars or in combat at a tournament are in several sets. Family life blissful or more often the reverse is plentiful, for instance the husband's return confronted with a wrathful wife swinging a skillet in his face is to be found in at least ten sets. There are scenes where the devil appears between two nuns or monks, listening to their conversation and tempting them from their religious duties.

Perhaps the subject both for popularity and representation are the incidents from the life of Reynard the Fox, a modern parallel being "Uncle Remus." Reynard and his companions fall into all sorts of scrapes due to over-reaching ambition and scheming. This fable is a political and ecclesiastical lampoon full of caustic gibes and cutting hits. At East Brent the fox is dressed as a bishop with staff and mitre preaching to the birds (151), principally geese, whom he afterwards kills and cooks upon a spit, Reynard is often dressed in a friar's garb for this act; his friend the monkey parading as a doctor is never far away; at York in the chapter-house he is whipping his cubs (142), on a stall at Ripon he wears a demure expression. On a corbel at Beverley St. Mary the hare dressed for hunting goes in pursuit of the dogs (144); it is a topsy-turvy world into which we are introduced, in which the aggressor often becomes the victim. Old saws are illustrated, at Whalley the blacksmith shoes the goose (158), with the motto that he who meddles with another's business shoes the goose; on a boss at Ugborough there is a blacksmith at work. Many quaint conceits are to be found, as on an elbow at Cartmel where a little dragon has been caught in a grin forming the letter T. Many stories and legends are illustrated but only those which had some message to convey. Some of the legends depicted have now been forgotten, but when carved were current fiction.

160 GRESFORD, DENBIGHSHIRE
162 BRISTOL, ST. MARY REDCLIFFE

161 MELTON-ON-THE-HILL, YORKSHIRE
163 BATTLEFIELD, SALOP

164 ABERGAVENNY, EVA CANTELUPE
165 HALTON HOLGATE, LINCS, UNKNOWN
166 HOLBEACH, LINCS, SIR HUMPHREY LITTLEBURY

HERALDIC DECORATION

"Art is doing the right thing in the right way, and beauty is the evidence of it."

W. R. LETHABY

WITH the commencement of the thirteenth century heraldry became an essentially important decoration. The interesting if arbitrary hieroglyphical signs used to designate various persons were placed upon their shields, which were blazoned in metals and primary colours; these later were surrounded by mantlings, helms, crests and supporters, forming a rich and varied adornment to the walls, roofs, chantry chapels, tombs, stained glass, woodwork, embroidery and tiles of both church and state; this was still further accentuated during the second half of the mediaeval period with its elaborations and repetitions. Early in the thirteenth century heraldry, or armour as it is called, had been reduced to a system, with a full classification and nomenclature of its own; and the various symbols and devices came to be regarded as the hereditary possessions of certain families or dignitaries of office.

During the earlier periods the English system was characterised by a delightful simplicity and freedom of drawing and style which continued down to Tudor times, when unfortunately it developed all sorts of complicated conceits which have been continued down to present days. Every type of device was charged or painted upon the shields, either singly or in combination: birds, beasts, fishes, flowers and fruits, everyday implements and garments or parts of them, such as heads, claws, wings, in addition to moons, suns, crescents, stars, *fleur-de-lys*, roundels, wheels; in fact everything under observation and many others which have never been seen were brought to the aid of the herald, who used them with telling effect. In filling a shield the craftsmen avoided monotony by not repeating the object either the same size nor even in quite the same form; if three lions were represented they were of various sizes to suit their positions on the shield, if three birds, the lowest is usually the largest, the object of this being to fill in the field without leaving awkward gaps and spaces, such as is now regularly found in the mechanical manner in which modern heraldry is treated. This pictorial language was coloured in red, blue, green, purple and black, combined with yellow for gold and white for silver, the ruling principle was that the two metals should not be superimposed nor if possible any other two colours. To quote Lethaby "The inimitable quality of these old charges came first from the spirit in which they were devised for a purpose, and from their perfect adjustments of drawing developed by frequent repetition. The beasts are marvels of fancy and have little relation to the waddling lions and boiled eagles of modern blazons."*

The shape of the shield varied during the centuries; in the twelfth it was kite-shaped with a long body, in the thirteenth it was shortened with an almost horizontal top. In the fourteenth the sides were straightened the kite shape disappearing, in the fifteenth the jousting shield came in with a deep notch for the lance rest on its right side. Later, shields were drawn with fanciful shapes and developed absurd exaggerated twists, curling over the top and bottom. In the fourteenth century the field was occasionally diapered, although this was independent of the charge proper; it was successfully used by glass painters and embroiderers as well as in stone and wood: perhaps its finest manifestation is on the Percy tomb at Beverley. In the second half of the time heraldry became so exact a science that the intermarriages of several generations could be shown by quarterings upon a single shield, subdivided several times, and also by marks of cadency, denoting which particular son was indicated; it is therefore possible, by a study of the impalements and quarterings of shields placed round a tomb, to read a fairly complete history of the family marriages in connection with the person commemorated. Nor were arms and devices confined to important families: the saints were given arms and emblems by which they could be easily recognised, shields often taking the place of representations of the saints, especially used in the tracery lights of a window, or upon the bosses of a vault. Cities also had the right to bear arms, together with societies and gilds, many of considerable antiquity; the Royal Arms of course taking precedence in its varied forms in England's long and chequered history.

Crests placed upon helms were at first used as a means of identification during battle, the face of the knight being hidden within his helm, and his arms painted upon his shield and embroidered upon his jupon too much lost to sight in the mêlée to be rightly observed. The crest was often a personal device, and in heraldry was placed above the shield, resting upon a twisted torse; this represented a piece of material wrapped round the helm to keep off the heat; it was also designed as a mantling to fill in the spaces round the shield, and was shown

* *Westminster and the King's Craftsmen*, page 366.

167 TOMB NORTH SIDE OF CHANCEL, NEWTON-BY-SUDBURY
168 ENRICHMENT FROM HITCHIN SCREEN

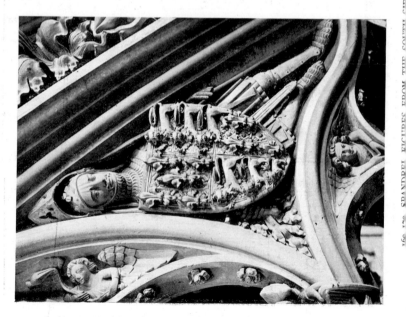

YORKSHIRE, RICHNESS IN FIGUREWORK AND HERALDRY

FIG. 172. SPANDREL FIGURES FROM THE SOUTH SIDE OF THE NAVE HTML

with dagged edges, possibly for the cuts received in battle. In addition to the torse outside the helm, there was also an inner torse or wreath between the helm and the bascinet to relieve the weight of the former. It is shown upon effigies as composed of velvet and pearls, studded in delightful designs, matching the netted caul worn by the ladies. Supporters do not appear before the third quarter of the fourteenth century; in the thirteenth century shields were shown hung from pegs or trees, sometimes from the neck of a bird or beast. Seals were perhaps responsible for supporters, the designers filling in the spaces with animals and birds. For some time supporters were varied and not standardised, and even after this took place changes could be made, the earl of Warwick having two muzzled bears with ragged staffs and also a bear and griffin. There is no doubt as to their decorative value; the Royal Arms would be less interesting and imposing if it were not for the lion and the unicorn.

In addition to the crest, there was also the badge which was worn by retainers and servants and was separate from the arms which were placed on the shield. When they first came into use is uncertain, but they were popular by the fourteenth century and lend themselves to artistic decoration and form an important addition to ordinary heraldry. The badge is a distinctive device used as a mark of cognisance of an individual or family, as the three ostrich feathers borne by the Prince of Wales as early as 1376 and found on the tomb of the Black Prince at Canterbury. The finest examples must surely be those used on the bronze doors of Henry VII's chapel, where they fill in the panels. In the thirteenth century the devices upon shields often bore some allusion to the name of the owner, and in later times this was taken a step further, especially in badges designed as a rebus or a punning allusion to the man's name, illustrated by the badge of abbot Islip at Westminster, representing an eye and a man falling out of a tree, or that of the abbot of Milton Abbas, a windmill standing upon a tun or barrel, and also the rams supporting the arms of abbot Ramryge on his chantry chapel at St. Albans (172).

Westminster abbey is a storehouse of early heraldry of the finest type, including the magnificent Royal Arms in the tiles of the chapter-house floor (178). There are eight existing shields in Henry III's quire aisles, two to each bay, hung from two small heads placed upon either side. Some have been destroyed by the blatant monuments with which the walls are crowded; those which survive however show how wonderfully the field is filled by the charges, especially the lions of England and

N

Ross, the single lions of Cornwall and Montford, and the arms of Empire, France, Warenne and that of St. Edward. Other shields of like character are on the unrivalled series of tombs beginning with Aveline wife of Crouchback 1273, Eleanor of Castile 1290, Crouchback 1296, William of Valance 1324, John of Eltham 1337, Philippa of Hainault 1369 and Edward III 1377. The shields of queen Eleanor are hung from small heads. At Chichester 1270 on the tomb of the countess of Arundel the surrounding shields are hung from bunches of foliage.

Many fine shields are carved with the effigies, both of knights and ladies; at Abergavenny, Eva de Cantelupe 1270 is covered by a large heater-shaped shield charged with three *fleur-de-lys* (164). William de Valance 1296 has a shield enriched with enamels, at Dodford, sir Robert de Keyes 1305 in Purbeck has a noble carved shield. Single lions are found upon the shield of a knight at Holton Holgate (165), Madoc ap Llewelyn ap Griffyn 1331 at Gresford, and sir John Lyon at Warkworth, 1346. Sir Humphrey Littlebury at Holbeach 1360 has two lions (166) and John of Eltham three. Other arms worthy of note are on the walls of the Berkeley chapel, Bristol 1309 and the nave walls at St. Albans; however the finest set are those on the canopy of the Percy tomb at Beverley 1340; they are held by a lady and seven knights, each filling a spandrel; they are well designed and superbly carved, the charges standing away from the field in an extraordinary manner (169, 170). With one exception the fields are diapered; one shield shows a chequering in which each alternate square is on a different level. In the thirteenth century and the early fourteenth, the miniature figures of relations were placed round the tomb with the shields either above or below them; the Chelleston quarry centre however introduced the shield-bearing angel standing within niches, first alternating with relatives but later occupying almost every niche (176); the ends of the tombs were often designed with two angels supporting a centre shield. Another form of decoration was the shield within a quatrefoil, as on the tomb of dean Gunthorpe 1498 at Wells and a tomb at Corsham, Wiltshire. There are delicately-cut shields of arms on the tomb of Henry FitzRoy, duke of Richmond, at Framlingham, 1536, and in the same church on the tomb of Thomas Howard, 3rd duke of Norfolk are delightful little rampant lions at each corner, holding shields. At Lanercost priory are two tombs in red sandstone to the Dacres 1526, the chest side with two angels holding arms, the centre panel, arms within a garter supported by salmon whose tails meet at the base. A fine example of mantling is carved upon the canopy over the effigy

171 ST. ALBANS, TOMB OF HUMPHREY DUKE OF GLOUCESTER, 1459
172 ST. ALBANS, CHANTRY OF ABBOT RAMRYGE, 1500
173 AUCKLAND CASTLE, ON ORIEL WINDOW

176 EWELME, OXON, DUCHESS OF SUFFOLK'S TOMB

175 HOLT, DENBIGHSHIRE, FONT

174 ST. ALBANS, DUKE OF GLOUCESTER'S TOMB, HAT OF MAINTENANCE

of sir John Spencer 1522, at Great Brington. Practically all tombs of fifteenth century date bear arms, and the custom was continued after the suppression, and was elaborated until it became possible to place sixty quarterings on a single shield, as that to the Booths, 1727 in Bowdon church, Cheshire.

Personal possessions such as the wearing of livery collars were shown upon effigies, the collars of esses, and suns and roses of Lancaster and York and the order of the Garter (78). In the later time knights' heads rest upon their helms surmounted by their crests, as the asses' head of the Mainwarings, the Turk's head of the de la Poles, the eagle and child of the Stanleys, the calf's head of the Calverleys and the Peacock of the Roos family; in the same way their feet often rested upon their badge, as the fish of sir Thomas Essex at Lambourne, the muzzled bear of the Warwicks and the rams at the feet of abbot Ralph of Ramsey. The tabard, a silk shirt over the armour, was worn during the fifteenth century; upon it were displayed the arms and badges of the person represented.

Chantry chapels were loaded with heraldry; Sugar's chantry at Wells has demi-angels on the cornice holding shields of the Passion and monograms, and abbot Ramryge's chantry at St. Albans has a series of arms of the dependent cells, each with his supporters, the collared ram (172). The Speke and Oldham chantries at Exeter are decorated in the same manner. A fine monument with superb heraldry is that to Humphrey, duke of Gloucester 1447 at St. Albans; here are shields, helms, mantlings, supporters and caps of maintenance, all in the latest luxurious vivid and free style of the period (171). At Exeter on the quire screens, angels support shields with the shroud, which elsewhere they had used for conveying the souls of the deceased to heaven.

Heraldry often became the principal decoration of gateways, oriels, and the exterior of buildings, whether castle or abbey. On the gateway at Butley priory are thirty-five shields in a panel over the doorway; other examples are at Kirkham priory and Peterborough and on the oriel window at Auckland castle (173). Shields were also used as pure decoration, round the chancel arches at Wingfield, Suffolk, and on the screen at Halse, Somerset. The motive is also occasionally found upon fonts, as at Holt, Denbigh (175) where the descent of the manor is given in arms and badges, and on a font at Winterbourne, Whitchurch. Magnificent collections of heraldry are to be found carved on the bosses of vaults, of which perhaps the finest is that of the Divinity School, Oxford, where there are not only arms and supporters but monograms and rebuses, such as the delightful little rampant lion holding on to 'el and producing Lionel. Many other vaults have large collections, especially in the cloisters of cathedrals and abbeys.

The rebus, playful and fanciful, is found in many places, the cocks of Bp. Alcock at Ely, the owls of Bp. Oldham at Exeter, the beacon and tun for Bp. Beckington at Wells as well as the hares at the feet of Bp. Harewell in the same place; the wheat ears for abbot Wheathamstead at St. Albans, the collar of palings round the neck of a Markenfield at Ripon, the Ox and ford for Oxford; these examples could be multiplied exceedingly. Heraldry humanised decoration, and gave it an additional interest, including family lore and tradition, and enriched the buildings with a pageantry of colour.

Heraldry, however, did not stop with masonry and tombs; it was used extensively in woodwork, glass, embroidery, tiles and metalwork; in fact it was adaptable to all materials, sizes and shapes, and is equally interesting in them all. In woodwork it is used on the noble stall-ends at Ripon, Manchester (89), Durham castle, Wensley and Aysgarth, also on the bench-ends found at Snittersfield, Monkleigh, Crowcombe, Bratoft and Fressingfield; the baberies at Beverley, Ottery and many other places have it, and the screens at Wensley, where it is mixed with the tracery, and Middleton, where it occupies the whole of the panelling with gorgeous mantlings; together with such panels still existing at Eastham, Cheshire, to give but a few examples of what may still be found. The glassworkers used it to great advantage, and many a glorious window contained little else but shields of arms and borders of badges (160–1). To go through the notebooks made by the four generations of the Randle Holmes' of Chester is to realise what wonderful collections of heraldry the church windows of a small county like Cheshire contained before the Civil Wars decimated the whole.

DECORATIVE FLOOR-TILES

"The human eye takes no aesthetic delight in perfection greater
than the human hand can achieve."

LOYD HABERLY, *Mediaeval English Paving-tiles*, page 1

FROM the twelfth century onwards a lowly type of decoration
in tiles was provided by craftsmen, which though intended to
be trodden under foot was one of importance. It was supplied
wherever it was thought desirable, such as in the sanctuary,
the subsidiary chapels, the chapter-house, or any other position
of dignity and reverence. This enrichment was provided by
tiles, either in self-colours and of varied shapes and sizes,
making it possible to design elaborate patterns by using differing
colours, such as have been found in the transepts of Byland
abbey, or of a patterned tile, impressed with an enrichment of
a secondary colour, the designs of which seem to be endless.
These designs include geometrical and arbitrary patterns, floral,
animal and figurework, heraldry and inscriptions, in addition
to tiles especially designed for borders and other requirements.
The colours produced were red, yellow, green and black, these
owing to the impurities of the chemicals employed were
liable to delightful variations of tint, as they were also in size,
preventing the dead monotony of the machine-made article.
The size depended not only on the quality of the clay, but on
its shrinkage while drying and baking, both seem to have been
of uncertain quantity.

Before the twelfth century floors were laid in slabs and
blocks of differently coloured stones as has been discovered
at Old Sarum during excavations of Bp. Roger's early twelfth
century cathedral, where white Chilmark alternated with green
Hurdcote stone. Throughout the whole time, flagging with
stone and marble, marking divisions and walks, was mingled
with the use of tiles. In the fifteenth century there was a return
to both stone and Purbeck marble for flooring, the tiles when
laid over a large area proving of poor wearing quality, owing
perhaps to their small size and uneven texture. The finest
periods of tile making were in the thirteenth and fifteenth
centuries, when in this later period a revival took place, which is
illustrated in the splendid series existing at Great Malvern priory.
As far as can be ascertained the Chertsey kilns produced the
best designed and finished products, although what is known of

their work has had to be gleaned from the fragmentary examples dug up first in 1853, which were afterwards stolen, and later in 1861. The one complete thirteenth century pavement *in situ* is that in the chapter-house at Westminster, of which the greater part of the tilework is genuine. Small collections are still to be found scattered in the majority of parish churches; unfortunately however these tiles have met with scant respect from either restorers or custodians and are generally much worn. The sites of conventual establishments have often proved a mine of wealth, especially Bordesley excavated 1866, Halesowen 1870 and Kenilworth 1922–3, but many sites had been rifled before they could be properly protected.

Although there were many sources of supply, the work in the majority of cases was of local origin. If the land proved suitable, as at Malvern, a local kiln was erected while the monastery was abuilding, which produced sufficient tiles to meet the requirements of the priory and the needs of the neighbouring churches, after which it would be shut down, for it was unlikely that the brethren would tolerate the smoke and fumes of a kiln so near to their completed buildings. There were of course many other places where tiles were made; the kilns at Malvern were found in 1833, Droitwich in 1837, Great Saredon in Staffordshire and Nottingham, and in 1911 an important kiln at Stoke near Coventry was unearthed. The various kilns varied in quality from the highly finished product both in design and workmanship to the coarsest clay and the unintelligent use of other men's designs.

For incised or decorated tiles it was essential that the kiln should be situated in the neighbourhood of a bed of white clay, now known as pipe clay, which was used for making the slip with which the designs were filled. It is local in its distribution whereas ordinary fireclay is fairly common. The method adopted for making tiles was to squeeze soft clay into wooden moulds, usually square in shape, with sloping sides, forming a small box. When the clay was turned out, still in a rather soft condition, it was impressed with a block of wood carved out to a given surface pattern, resembling a butter print. The clay was then left to dry until it was ready to receive the white slip which was well mixed with water and filled up the hollows of the design; the tiles were then placed in a shed to dry, but before firing in the kiln were sprinkled over with lead ore which when cool gave a metallic glaze, turning the white to yellow and giving the red a richer hue. The ordinary black tiles were coloured with manganese, the white covered with slip, both usually finished with lead-ore glaze.

PROBABLY FROM THE CHERTSEY KILNS AND OF THE FINEST QUALITY

177, 178 TILES FROM THE FLOOR OF WESTMINSTER CHAPTER-HOUSE, 1253–1259

180 GLOUCESTER CATHEDRAL

179 BROADWAS, WORCESTERSHIRE

In decorated tiles several designs formed a single unit which could be repeated as often as desired or counterchanged at will: however in the finer class of work it took several tiles to form a pattern, either in twos, threes, fours, nines or sixteens as the case might be. Borders had a starting tile, an intermediate and a finishing tile so that the intermediate could be repeated as often as required, such as the tree growing out of the mouth of a mask at Maxstoke castle. Tiles were occasionally employed as grave covers, as at Lingfield and Effingham, Surrey, the tiles being 15 inches square with a green glaze. Tiles were sometimes used for wall decoration as in the unique set at Gt. Malvern which are inscribed, and dated 1457–8. These consist of five tiles; the first from the base has the Pelican in her Piety placed on a treetop: the second the arms of England and France quarterly, the third an I.H.S. and crown, the fourth a shield of the Passion, and the top tile a canopy with pinnacles in imitation of the glassworkers.

The Chertsey tiles, the finest ever discovered in England, were evidently used at Westminster. Many designs are also found at Halesowen, which was founded by the duke of Cornwall, though there is a difference in the manufacture of the latter. At Chertsey they produced two series of tiles illustrating the legends of Richard Cœur de Lion and Tristram and Iseult which may be dated 1270. The Westminster chapter-house floor was laid rather earlier, between 1253–9, and contains the portraits of Henry III, his queen Eleanor and Archbp. Crokesley, the Confessor giving his ring to St. John, musicians and hunting scenes, first the king on horseback with his dog, second an archer with strung bow, and third the stag and hound, together with a magnificent representation of the Royal Arms (177–8). A border illustrates St. Peter's salmon, the fishes facing each other in pairs. The Chertsey kiln produced separate letters on wedgeshaped small tiles for inscriptions to fit circles of any size. There are hunting scenes elsewhere at Romsey and Lewes; knights on horseback fully armed and going the pace are found at Gloucester and at Cleeve;—it is suggested that the two opposing knights are Richard and Saladin. At Notley a tile shows a hare under an oak bush and there are tiles with three hares, their single ears forming the central triangle. At Little Marlow is a billman, and many other such subjects are shown. Tiles lend themselves particularly to the decorative qualities of coats-of-arms, of which there are hundreds of examples, used either singly or in groups; both kinds are at Gloucester (180). At Tewkesbury a design of sixteen tiles contains four muzzled bears and four shields, and at Malvern a set illustrating the descent of the manor in much the same way as does the font at Holt, Denbigh. There is an interesting rebus at Worcester of Bp. Tydeman of Winchcomb, 1395–1401, it represents a capstan with a rope wound round it, behind which is a double comb crowned with a mitre and pastoral staff. Sets of tiles with inscriptions are common, both memorial and invocatory: there are also lines of poetry, alphabets, humorous proverbs, charms against fire and even contempt for executors, the last two originally in Holy Trinity church Stratford-on-Avon.

Other forms of tiles included the raised or moulded design (181–2), used where white clay was difficult to obtain, and an expensive type with sgraffito technique. This type was engraved by hand through a coat of white slip so that the figures stood out from the red ground; as only one could be made of each design they were used for very special work, where the cost was of no account. There was a set at Tring church, but these have been divorced from their setting, with the sequence broken up, and are hidden away in two museums.

WHERE PIPECLAY WAS ABSENT, TILES RECEIVED MODELLED DESIGN

182 ABBEY DORE, HEREFORDSHIRE

181 LAUNCELLS, CORNWALL

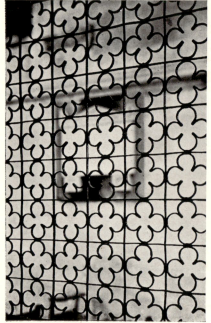

183 LINCOLN CATHEDRAL
184 CHICHESTER CATHEDRAL

185 WINCHESTER CATHEDRAL
186 CANTERBURY, ST. ANSELM'S CHAPEL

METALWORK

"It is the part of every good workman to produce what is required of him in the best possible manner—to do otherwise is merely to stultify himself and eventually to lose his place among the craftsmen of other trades."

"It is this childlike disregard for symmetry and order which lends much charm to the early work. Such lapses become more and more rare as time advances, and the education which minimised them was too often accompanied by loss of individuality and life."

Wrought Iron by MAXWELL AYRTON and ARNOLD SILCOCK, pp. 27–30

THE craft of the metalworker includes that of the goldsmith and silversmith, the workers in bronze, laton and iron, as well as the armourer, and the founders of bells and casters of brass; it is a subject which includes many varieties of work from the minute to the massive, and, from the plain to a filigree of delicate loveliness, all are included in the art of the metal-worker. Unfortunately we have but scattered descriptions by mediaeval writers to help us to picture the creative work done in precious metals, the value of the material carrying with it the seeds of its own destruction; this has been as thorough as if the Nazis had been given the work to do, and from much the same motive, greed and malice in equal parts. Imperishable as metal is, the greater part of the mediaeval work in metal has vanished, the shrines, images, and vessels at the suppression, the grilles and screens at two distinct periods, the Reformation and the nineteenth century restoration period, when the grilles and grates surrounding tombs were torn down by the hundred, and with less excuse than the recent raids upon exterior railings. Bronze effigies have been broken up, engraved brasses melted down, practically everything of value either purloined, stolen or dispatched under some specious guise, but in every case to fill the pockets of nefarious persons at the expense of the church. What is left however is sufficient to gauge the crafts-manship of the bronze founder and the ironworker during his three periods of activity and surprising success.

The smiths of early Britain were too fully engaged in forging weapons of war, and in making chain-mail and other defensive materials, to be seriously occupied with religious crafts, and it was not until the twelfth century that door hinges of an elaborate nature became part of their output. Mr. Starkie Gardner has

97   o

stated that the English smith was in the forefront of Europe and maintained that eminence well into the fourteenth century. In spite of neglect and restoration there are still a series of doors covered with elaborate whorls and complicated twists made by these ingenious smiths. Their designs are extraordinarily varied and suggest several origins, such as the Viking ships at Stillingfleet, the Swastikas at Skipwith (187), and the ducks and eels at Worfield. The main hinges were generally crescent shaped for strength, otherwise the majority of the ironwork was decorative, and used in keeping the boarding together, as in the door at Durham 1135, which is closely packed with ornamental scrollwork. By the thirteenth century ironwork was fashioned into delicate vine growths and whorls, exemplified iu the west door of Henry III's chapel at Windsor (188), the chapter-house at York and the south door at Worksop.

The ironworkers were also employed upon grilles and grates for all churches possessing treasures, especially shrines which gradually became encrusted with gold and precious stones. The earliest example now remaining is at Winchester, dated about 1100 (185), formerly protecting the shrine of St. Swithun, a fragment of which is now at the west end of the nave. These screens were more in the way of a spider's web, delicately designed so as not to interrupt the view, but intended as a protection; nevertheless they had little constructional value, the different pieces held in position by welded collars and not forged as a whole; other grilles of a like type are still at Lincoln (183), Canterbury (186) and Chichester (184), and these four fragments are probably all that are left from the hundreds of early screens which formerly filled in and protected the valuables of the abbeys, cathedrals and churches of England. In the same way as the grilles, the candelabra, lecterns and font-cranes have all disappeared.

By the close of the thirteenth century smithing had attained to a position which was almost unrivalled. With the decrease of military needs more attention was paid to refinement in craftsmanship and design and this particularly affected the ironworker. In 1294 Thomas de Leighton was employed to make a grille for the tomb of queen Eleanor, as a protection against thieves climbing over the effigy into the feretory, and admirably it fulfils its task (8). It commences at the height of the tomb chest, bowing forward and finishing in tridents. It consists of eleven openwork panels of whorls and foliage similar to those attached to doors, the whole welded together in a masterly manner without distortion, and is one of the finest pieces of smithing of its period in Europe. Thomas is supposed

RAPID ADVANCE OF SMITHING SHOWN BY THESE TWO EXAMPLES IN THE THIRTEENTH AND EARLY FOURTEENTH CENTURIES

188 ST. GEORGE'S, WINDSOR, EARLY DOOR

187 SKIPWITH DOOR, YORKSHIRE

189 ASHOVER.   190 WAREHAM AND 191 FRAMPTON-ON-SEVERN

to have been a native of Leighton Buzzard, the doors at the church there having certain characteristics of his style. At Chester is a large cope cupboard which has many affinities to the Eleanor grille, and is probably the work of the same smiths; the process was mainly the result of stamping dies on the hot iron, the curves made by moulding irons. Other chests were enriched with flowing scrolls, such as those at Westminster abbey, the York cope chests, and parish church chests found at Malpas, Audlen and elsewhere, generally local copies of better-class work.

The craft of the smith apart from the worker in iron needs defining; his tools were few, an anvil, hammer, fire and bellows, and with these he had to produce speedily, while the iron was red-hot, whatever shape he had in mind—no time here for delicate adjustments or symmetrical accuracy, but a direct expertness of hand and eye, with a freedom and simplicity of curve which is the charm of thirteenth-century design; along with this is a strong note of individuality and an adaptability to meet the needs of the material and the difficulties of spacing, thereby avoiding the monotony so apparent in modern work; in fact the expression "machine-made" work carries with it a hostile criticism on any craftsman's work, even at the present day when machines are the gods of this mechanically minded generation.

With the fourteenth century the work of the smith altered to meet new conditions and requirements, it became sober in style and simple in form. This is well illustrated in the tomb grates which came into fashion with the elevation of the effigy upon a tomb chest, especially during the alabaster period. The grates took several forms, simple uprights threaded through crossbars and finishing in spikes, as round the Swinford tomb 1371 at Spratton, or in the forms of a hearse, as at Bunbury round the Calverley tomb 1416, the Marmion tomb 1387 at West Tanfield (202), or the magnificent laton hearse over the figure of Richard Beauchamp 1464 at Warwick (196). The decorative qualities of these vertical grates was enhanced by the treatment of the standards and the top horizontal bar. This is shown in great completeness in the Hungerford tomb 1398 where the horizontal bars are pierced and the top edge serrated, the standards with elaborate sawn iron foliage (199), the verticals instead of spikes have alternating designs of *fleur-de-lys* with Maltese crosses and pear-shaped spikes. The grates of the Arundel tomb 1415 and the Beckington tomb at Wells 1465 have battlemented crossbars, the standards elaborately buttressed, the heads moulded octagonally with sprickets. The

Wells grate has a double bar, the lower pierced with quatrefoils, decorated with shields and busts of the bishop.

As already stated the smith altered his methods during the fourteenth century to suit new conditions and treated his material not so much as malleable metal, but as if it were timber, sawing and cutting it when cold and fitting it together, for iron may be sawn into delicate shapes with extreme accuracy, and this "benchwork" attained a high degree of proficiency and perfection, as seen in the grates for the chapel of Henry V at Westminster and the chapel of Edward IV at Windsor (12). Other beautiful decorative work consisted of door-fittings, lock-plates, door handles and key scutcheons (192–5), to be found in the Beauchamp chapel, Warwick and St. George's, Windsor (13). These decorative locks are used for chests as the ones at Crediton and East Dereham, though possibly these may be of continental origin.

The finest example of ornamental ironwork produced during the mediaeval period is that at Windsor to the chapel of Edward IV (13). It is the work of John Tresilian, principal smith to Windsor Castle from 1477 onwards. It is in the richest style of fifteenth-century architecture, worked out in full relief down to the minutest detail, and embraces two gates with tall attendant towers. Thousands of pieces have gone into its construction, all carefully sawn and cut, tenoned, morticed and riveted together. Depth and richness are obtained by using one thickness upon another of saw-pierced sheet iron, and the intricacy of detail produced by this process is remarkable (13). The caps, bases, mouldings, crockets and cusps are traced out in the solid; the whole was originally gilt. The grate for Henry V was erected in the reign of Henry VII, and when first put up was ornamented with *fleur-de-lys*, lions, and an alternating row of swans and antelopes, the whole coloured and gilt. The tomb of Henry VII is surrounded by a gilt laton screen unfinished in 1509. It is London work; Lethaby describing says: "it is an extraordinarily beautiful work, one of the most masterly pieces of metal casting in Europe. It is conceived with great frankness as a little building of brass, all of open-work lattices, traceries and brattishings, with turretlike projections at the corners, all the details sharp and vivid; and the inscriptions, badges of greyhounds and red dragons and images are triumphs of skill." The small images were the work of Lawrence Imber of London; only six of them now remain.

BRONZE CASTING.—Bronze or laton was used during the whole mediaeval period, and fortunately there remain ten effigies cast in this material which illustrate this work during

192 GLOUCESTER, ST. NICHOLAS   193 STOKE LYME
194 NORWICH CATHEDRAL   195 BOSTON GILDHALL

196 WARWICK, ST. MARY, BEAUCHAMP CHAPEL, TOMB OF RICHARD BEAUCHAMP,
EARL OF WARWICK, A.D. 1457. MADE IN PURBECK MARBLE AND LATON

197, 198 DETAILS OF THE TOMB TO SIR RICHARD BEAUCHAMP AT WARWICK

METALWORK IN TOMB GRATES, LECTERNS, HOURGLASSES

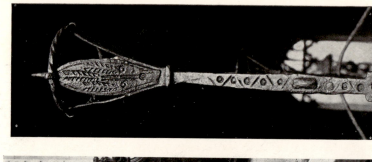

202 WEST TANFIELD
TOMB STANDARD

201 WIGGENHALL ST. M. V., BRASS
LECTERN

200 COMPTON BASSET, HOURGLASS

199 FARLEIGH HUNGERFORD
TOMB STANDARD

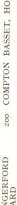

nearly four hundred years, and include some of the finest examples of figurework and casting to be found in Europe, The earliest are the effigies of Henry III and his queen, Eleanor (1292) the work of William Torel, goldsmith of London, and were a first attempt at casting large figures by the waste-wax system. Their attitude is noble and stately and the figure of the queen is the perfection of beauty. The surface is engraved with designs then in use for the decoration of gesso surfaces, the costumes enriched with glass and gems. The casting of the series of effigies which follow is superb; they include Edward III (1377), his son Edward prince of Wales (1376) (79) and of Richard II and his consort Anne of Bohemia (1395). These last were by Nicholas Broker and Godfrey Prest, citizens of London; the indenture included two images in metal-gilt of the king and queen, placed upon a metal table, gilt and ornamented with a fretwork of *fleur-de-lys*, lions, eagles and leopards. Over their heads were gables of gilt metal, with two lions at the feet of the king and an eagle and leopard at the feet of the queen. Twelve images of saints were to be placed round about the tomb and eight angels attending the king and queen; the metalwork was to cost four hundred pounds. The tomb of Richard Beauchamp, earl of Warwick, who died in 1439, was not set up until eighteen years after his death (196–8). It is one of the most perfect and sumptuous which have come down to us. William Austin, founder and Thomas Stevyns coppersmith covenanted for the effigy, and Bartholomew Lambspring, Dutchman and goldsmith, covenanted to clean, gild, burnish and polish the great image of laton and other ornaments, the whole work to be "of the finest latton, the work in the most finest wise and gilded with the finest gold." The effigies of Henry VII and Elizabeth of York were contracted for in 1512 by Humfrey Walker, founder, and Nicholas Ewen, coppersmith and gilder, to be made under the direction of Peter Torregiano of the city of Florence, carver and painter. Torregiano was also responsible for the effigy of Lady Margaret Beaufort, countess of Richmond and Derby for her tomb (1511) in Westminster abbey. Many other figures which were cast in bronze have disappeared including one to lord Derby (1509), formerly in Ormskirk church, Lancs. Other methods of decoration in metal were employed, as the Limoges enamelled plates used to cover the wooden effigy of William de Valance (1296), and the destroyed tomb to Walter de Merton. Silver plates were used in a similar way for the effigy of Henry V at Westminster, but were soon stolen.

Another form of memorial was the engraved laton plate, of which it is computed that at least 150,000 were laid down during the mediaeval period and of which even now about 3,000 remain. The plates were made in Flanders and Cologne and were called "Cullen" plates. The metal was cast in sheets of the required size and imported to England to be engraved in this country. The continental engraver covered the whole of his background with ornament; the English artist however allowed the figure to stand out from the background. The method of engraving was different, the continental artist using a broad-shaped chisel, the Englishman a burin or lozenge-shaped graver, allowing greater freedom of execution and a more vigorous line. The centre of the craft was in London, and there is a distinct link between the bronze effigy makers and the engravers. The distribution of brasses follows well-marked lines, the greatest number in the home counties, along the east coast, and in the south-west. The earliest brasses, laid down in the late thirteenth and early fourteenth centuries, are as excellent as anything produced later. The figures are nearly life-size, many of them enriched with beautiful canopies. Floriated crosses, a form peculiar to England, were largely used, especially for ecclesiastics and civilians, many of exquisite design. The brasses of the first half of the fifteenth century are remarkable for the carefulness of their execution, cross shading being employed. By the end of the century figures tend to become a little stiff, the shading overdone and the general level of excellence declined. With the dawn of the sixteenth century the decline was rapid, attempts were made to treat the subject pictorially and the renaissance proved a disturbing factor without producing any fresh artistic influence.

BRASS OR LATON CASTING.—This was not confined either to the continent or to post-reformation England, for over forty examples of brass lecterns have survived to the present day, and the majority bear unmistakable evidence of their English character and origin (201). Where however they were manufactured or the names of the founders is as yet unknown, but judging by their distribution eastern England was probaby the site of the foundries, for twenty-one remain there, while only three are in the home counties. They all bear a family likeness and like the eighteenth-century candelabra their parts were often interchangeable, such as wings, feet, and the little lions supporting the standard. They could be altered when engraving the details and feathers and made to appear different. The standard is composed of a circular shaft with numerous mouldings, a widespreading base, the top completed with a

THE WORK OF WILLIAM EDNEY OF BRISTOL, ERECTED 1710

203, 204 ST. MARY REDCLIFFE, BRISTOL. FORMERLY THE CHANCEL SCREEN, NOW AT THE WEST END

THE WORK OF WILLIAM EDNEY OF BRISTOL. DESTROYED BY THE NAZIS

205 SWORD REST AND 206 RAILS, TEMPLE CHURCH

207 2ND SWORD REST,

large ball upon which stood the eagle. In four cases the top is completed by a double desk and although no example survives there were four-sided lecterns made for the great abbeys. Occasionally the eagle of St. John is exchanged for the Pelican in its Piety as at Norwich, but this example is probably of Flemish manufacture. Practically all these lecterns are of fifteenth century date; earlier lecterns seem to have been made of timber, and of course the patterns used by the founders were first cut for his use by the woodcarver, and when cast still often suggest their origin. Casting was in use from early times, but with the exception of one or two bells little has come down to us; however there is a fine bronze-cast mortar now in the York museum which was dug up on the site of St. Mary's abbey and is dated 1308.

Lead and tin were products of Britain from early times and the use of the former has been general for churchwork, for roofs, gutters, drainage and even for fonts of which about forty remain, in spite of the temptation to melt them into bullets for destroying in place of baptising mankind. There are two principal types; those which are cast in a single piece as the one at Wareham (190) and those which were made of flat sheets of lead, with repeated cast ornaments, the sheets then bent round and soldered to form a cylinder; all lead fonts stand upon stone bases or pedestals. Their provenance is in the south of the country and there is little doubt that they were made in England. The favourite design is an arcade of semi-circular arches on piers with caps and bases, housing figures either standing as at Wareham, seated as at Dorchester, Oxon, or alternating with scrollwork as at Frampton-on-Severn (191); the figurework at Dorchester, Wareham, Walton-on-the-Hill and Lower Halston is excellent. A small font at Brookland, Kent, is decorated with the signs of the zodiac, illustrated by scenes of labours appropriate to each month of the year. At Barnet-le-Wolde the font has three bands of twelfth century foliated ornament. Practically all the important lead fonts are of either twelfth or thirteenth century date, after which they are sporadic; the last made in the seventeenth century is at Clunbridge in Gloucestershire.

CHURCH CRAFTSMANSHIP AFTER THE SUPPRESSION

"If there is an injustice to set right, a fool to be removed, do it if you can, for the evil works of the fool live after him. But I have come to the conclusion that the love of beauty and excellence is abnormal, and that the world is intended for fools. It therefore behoves us to fight for what we want, we shall not get it otherwise."

Self Portrait, CHARLES RICKETTS

THE suppression brought with it a break between church and craftsmanship; the minds of those in authority were too busily engaged upon destruction and the question of material gain to themselves to give a thought as to what became of the trade in church furnishings. The lay mind had always lagged in things pertaining to beauty as compared with the ecclesiastical world, in fact the veneer of civilisation was even thinner than it is today, and it required but a scratch to produce the savage; we have an illustration of this at the present time in the Nazi mind, which though not unintelligent, has under malign influence become brutalised, shedding its civilisation as easily as a snake sheds its skin.

Some crafts survived the shock; others as quickly died out or were diverted into secular channels such as furniture, metal-work, embroidery and tomb-making, this last a contribution to the self-aggrandisement of the family of the lord of the manor, with the monuments emblazoned with their arms and connections. It became essential in Elizabeth's reign to restore some sort of law and order into the church, and the re-furnishing of the interiors began; Holy Tables, rails, pulpits, galleries and other necessary things were installed, and until the advent of the Commonwealth this was continued, the fabrics repaired and the roofs renewed. Neither the tomb-maker or the carpenter ever lost touch with his materials; the latter was employed in the erection of the fine timbered mansions which were required for those persons who had greatly profited by the downfall of the monasteries. In much the same way the metalworker was called upon to furnish gates and railings to enclose these new demesnes, and there was a renaissance of his work of the first order: he also later contributed his quota to the church in the form of screens, communion rails and other furniture. A short review of these varied later activities connected with the churches will complete the story of the craftsmanship which we have been considering.

POST-REFORMATION MONUMENTS.—With Henry VIII's break with Rome the English tradition of tomb-making came to a close; although it had changed in materials and style it had remained homogeneous in inspiration and outlook; even after 1500 it refused to be influenced by continental fashions which had long embraced the revival of classical learning and architecture. The attempt made by the Court to introduce Italian ideals and individual sculptors found no root in English soil; its surface ornament might be superimposed upon native construction, but with the severance from Rome even that ceased, and was gradually supplanted by the growing commercial relations with the Netherlands, causing the real break from English tradition. This influence was propagated by the large number of Flemish artists and sculptors who, settling in England, seldom returned to their native land. Although termed "aliens" they received the greater share of the patronage of the time, to the detriment of the native firms.

The Midland shops near the alabaster quarries continued their production of tombs and effigies for another fifty years, Robert Parker, "alablasterer" of Burton-on-Trent, doing fine work. He was responsible for the tomb of Thomas, 1st earl of Rutland at Bottesford, 1543. This shows but little change in format, with the exception of minor details of decoration and the absence of nichework round the sides of the tomb. Other existing examples of this school and time are the monuments to sir Thomas Bromley, 1555, at Wroxeter; sir Thomas Cave, 1558, at Stanford-on-Avon; and sir Thomas Andrews and his two wives at Charwelton, Northamptonshire, 1564. These tombs were among the last flowering of mediaeval tradition; the remaining work of these years, principally by the Roylances of Burton and kindred shops, show a continuous deterioration of workmanship both in style and execution—the effigies become clumsy, weak-kneed, poorly proportioned, and the details of the tombs were not only roughly cut, but the very meaning of the forms displayed obliterated.

By the end of the century the Midland firms seem to have closed down through lack of work, and by the wanton destruction of tombs in the reigns of Edward VI and Elizabeth, which discouraged further erection of tombs until the country became more settled. In the meanwhile however the London shops became serious rivals of the Midland centres. These sculptors, nearly all aliens, were free from English tradition, and although they continued the use of alabaster, it was combined with

P

various foreign marbles, black touch and slate. In format, tradition held for a time, and the aliens were compelled to conform to the use of the tomb chest and the recumbent pose for figures. Many tombs were still constructed free and independent, but more and more were they placed against a wall, often recessed, and surmounted by a classic canopy. The classical architectural detail of these sixteenth and seventeenth century tombs is by no means pure, judged by the standards of today; but it cannot be denied that what they lack in purity they gain in interest. The juggling with elements of the classic styles is for ever amusing, more human and alive than the hidebound rigid severity of the pure and unadulterated work. The work of the Netherland school is more flamboyant, richer in light and shade, and more suitable to the starched ruffs, the abundant wigs, and the voluminous garments of the ladies, than that of the mediaeval period; nevertheless it lacked its cultured refinement and repose. The mediaeval effigies give the impression of trust in quiescent tranquillity; that of the post-Reformation effigies, of complacency or repressed energy, of the earth earthy.

The mediaeval tradition of colour lingered on during the sixteenth and seventeenth centuries, notwithstanding the rising antagonism of the puritan elements, who associated anything colourful or beautiful with popery; this being an additional reason for the destruction of many tombs during the Civil Wars. It was in this period that portraiture became fashionable; in mediaeval times a ready-made tomb with the effigies of a knight and a lady was all that was considered necessary, excepting under very special circumstances. A new feature was the kneeling figure, very rare before the sixteenth century, an exception being Edward, lord Despencer, at Tewkesbury, 1370-80. This pose was adapted for weepers or children, who, in place of standing within niches, facing outwards, were now placed upon a narrow platform before the tomb, kneeling upon cushions facing the heads of the effigies. Later, the kneeling pose was used for the principal figures, especially for wall tombs, where they kneel at prayer desks facing each other.

Heraldry, which had always played an important part in the decoration of tombs, now gained still further importance; the ramifications of the family alliances and their connections became linked up in quarterings and impalements innumerable. Shields, crests, and supporters were blazoned on the conspicuous parts of the monuments; so much so that together with the inscriptions, it is possible to read a family history. In mediaeval days the inscription was of the shortest, giving the names of

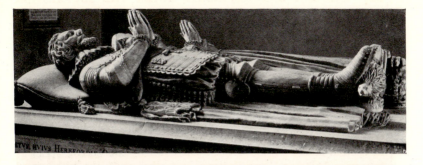

208 MUCH MARCLE, HEREFORDSHIRE, SIR JOHN KYRLE, Bt., 1650
209 BRAMFIELD, SUFFOLK, ELIZABETH COKE, 1634, BY N. STONE
210 ELMLEY CASTLE, WORCESTERSHIRE, E. SAVAGE, 1631

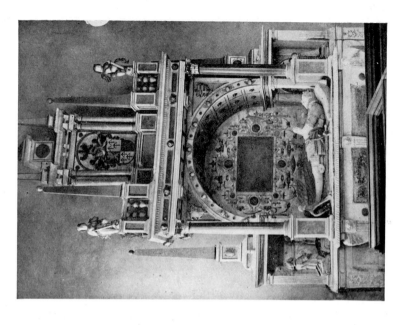

212 BREDON, WORCESTERSHIRE, GILES REED, 1611

211 REDGRAVE, SUFFOLK, SIR JOHN HOLT, 1709

the deceased, the dates of their obit and a prayer to God for
their souls. After the suppression inscriptions became constantly longer and more diffuse, recording not only the names
and dates, but including all the dignities, attainments and
qualities of the deceased, and actually laying claim to a notable
place in the heavens, where as at Gawsworth in Cheshire on a
tomb to the Fittons, 1619, is the following: "Whose soules and
bodys beauties sentance them Fittons to weare a heavenly
diadem." The outlook in a hundred years had suffered a total
change; no longer were there representations of Our Lord,
the Blessed Virgin and the Saints, but of the abstract virtues
possessed by the deceased, faith, hope, charity, learning and
wisdom; these figures decorate the pediments and grace the
sides of many tombs. Again, owing to the interest taken in the
exploration of fresh continents, figures of Indians and woodmen
were carved, as on the tomb of the duchess of Suffolk 1580,
at Spilsby. Later, symbolism ran riot and the tombs were
crowded with weeping cherubs holding doused torches, skulls
with cross-bones, hour-glasses, scythes and urns, all forming
part of the scheme of decoration.

As the old tradition died out other poses for effigies came
into fashion, the recumbent figure stirring into life, leaning
upon an elbow, sitting, kneeling and standing (later in rather
theatrical attitudes) surrounded by graceful figures of grief,
justice and mercy, as on the monument to Judge Holt, 1709
at Redgrave, Suffolk (211). The classic mode unhappily did not
stay at the architectural background, but extended to the
costume of the effigy. As early as 1670 we find the 8th earl of
Rutland clothed in a Roman toga with bare legs, his feet
enclosed in sandals, which later, combined with a wig, became
a current mode of presentation. With the effigy we may add the
wall monument, with either busts or medallions; there is a
fine example by Nicholas Stone at York, 1615 (213), and a
double one at Stanton Harcourt 1688, by Edward Marshall of
Oxford, showing a combination of wreaths, cherubs, urns and
drapery. The last is never inspiring and occasionally ludicrous,
where as at St. Mark's, Bristol, 1667, are two kneeling figures
pulling away curtains from a central niche, revealing a frightened
lady, Dame Mary Baynton with her two sons, probably by
Caius Gabriel Cibber.

By the second half of the seventeenth century, the use of
white marble became general, together with greater freedom
of treatment; this was especially noticeable in the way children
were depicted. To the close of the sixteenth century they were
presented as miniature adults, an exception being with a young

Stanley at Elford 1470, who was killed by being hit by a tennis ball behind the ear. One of the earlier monuments is to Henry Cookin, aged 11 in St. Mark's Bristol, 1627 (214), where he is shown as a schoolboy, the pilasters decorated with pens, inkpots and books. Other examples include Francis Gamul, 1620 who kneels at the feet of his mother at St. Mary's, Chester, and the delightful baby with a nosegay at Tarporley, Mary Knightley, who died at the age of thirteen months and was buried with her granny. By 1791 the freedom of presentation was complete, shown by Banks at Ashbourne to Penelope Boothby, an only child aged six. "She was in form and intellect, most exquisite, the unfortunate parents ventured their all on this frail bark and the wreck was total."

Among the many foreign names which confront us in connection with monumental sculpture stands that of a Devon man named Nicholas Stone, son of a quarryman, who when he grew up set up for himself in London. Fortunately his account books have survived, and it is possible to trace the greater number of his works. He died in 1647 leaving a fine tradition behind him. With the passing of the shopwork, sculptors produced their monuments in their studios with assistants who "ghosted" for them; this encouraged individuality of style and by the close of the seventeenth century carvers began to sign their work. These names include Francis Bird, 1667–1731; Peter Scheemakers, 1690–1771; Henry Cheeres, 1703–81; the theatrical Roubiliac, who died in 1762; Nollekens 1737–1823 and others. The Stantons of three generations should be included, the middle generation producing the remarkable monuments at Gt. Mitton, Lancashire and Tarporley, Cheshire, both in 1698. Towards the close of the eighteenth century the Attic mode became fashionable, produced by Flaxman and carried on by Gibson and Chantry. By the middle of the nineteenth century design had ceased to count; in the eighteenth the art of lettering was excellent, and it is deplorable that taste fell to such depths in the following century. The dreadful lettering of the monumental masons at the present time is quite shocking. The better class memorial such as the one to Charlotte Egerton 1845 at Rostherne, is sugary and sentimental, lacking the sweet simplicity and dignity of Penelope Boothby of 1791.

POST-REFORMATION WOODWORK.—The case of the ecclesiastical woodworker was a little different to that of the tomb-maker; he had ruled the fashion in secular woodwork during the latter half of the mediaeval period, but with its close it was the designer of domestic furniture who controlled church fittings. Mediaeval tradition quickly died, and but for a short revival

215 LANREATH, CORNWALL
WOODEN MONUMENT TO
CHARLES GRYLLS, 1623

214 ST. MARK'S, BRISTOL, HENRY COOKIN,
AGED 11, 1627

213 YORK CATHEDRAL
BY NICHOLAS STONE TO
ANNE BENNET, 1615

216 DRAYTON HOUSE, NORTHANTS, CHAPEL REREDOS

217 THE ORGAN CASE, ST. LAWRENCE JEWRY, LONDON
DESTROYED BY GERMAN INCENDIARY BOMBS, CHRISTMAS 1940

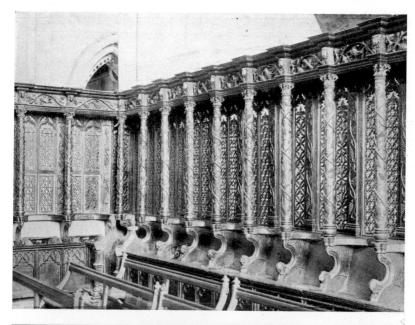

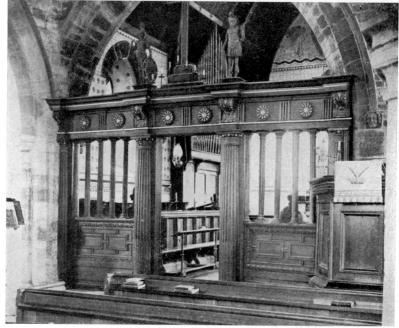

218 CARTMEL PRIORY STALL CANOPIES, 1620
219 HOLDENBY, NORTHANTS, CHANCEL SCREEN, 1580

in the seventeenth century was never again either copied or used as inspiration until the nineteenth century restorations. The making of screens and stalls was now the exception not the rule, the joiners devoting themselves to the construction of tables, rails, pulpits, pewing and galleries, all domestic in character. The furnishings of the Elizabethan age bore little relation to the refined and delicate work of the earlier period, rather they followed the style of the Netherlands and were massive, cumbrous and coarse, as is seen in the heavy bulbous legs of the tables, the rails of which were overcrowded with shallow repeat patterns, that also formed the decoration for pulpits, chairs, chests and wherever surface patterning could possibly be introduced. This furniture was strong in timbering but rarely graceful and less often beautiful. By the close of the seventeenth century twisted turnings appear, producing some degree of elegance and lightness, which was accompanied by jewel drop ornaments and sunk panel mouldings; as the Commonwealth approached however, there was a marked decline, the furniture becoming commonplace in design and its making almost ceased until after the Restoration.

During the period just discussed Archbishop Laud spent part of his life in an endeavour to restore some degree of dignity and order to the Anglican church. His example was instrumental in causing further efforts to be made by a few persons whose labours deserve our respect and admiration. Unfortunately with but few exceptions this has been the missing note of modern restoration, their work having been contemptuously turned out. John Harrison of Leeds, finding the needs of the populace uncared for, built the church of St. John at his sole cost in 1604, and furnished it with screens, pewing and pulpit. George Preston of Holker hall re-roofed the quire of Cartmel priory in 1620, and placed elaborate canopies over the existing stalls as well as a set of screens. George Herbert restored the church of Leighton Bromswold in Huntingdonshire in 1626. Viscount Scudamore in 1634 re-roofed the quire and transepts of the Cistercian abbey of Dore, furnishing the church with screen, pulpit and fittings. The work at Leeds and Abbey Dore is Jacobean in character, but the Cartmel canopies (218), coming between them, have a classical feeling of the early renaissance. For the genesis of the work we may turn to Scotland which for some time before the suppression had been under French influence. This type filtered across the border and is to be found both at Carlisle and Hexham.

With the Restoration of Charles II, this excellent work was continued under Bishop Cosin, who in 1665 replaced the destroyed stallwork in Durham cathedral, surmounting it with tabernacled canopies full of mediaeval feeling; he also placed a dignified pulpitum across the quire and screens round St. Cuthbert's feretory, all of which were ignominiously destroyed in 1846. It is interesting to note that Dr. Cosin preached the opening sermon in Harrison's church at Leeds, and later erected a fair screen, now also destroyed, in the University church of Gt. St. Mary, Cambridge, where he was vice-chancellor; he further adorned the church of Brancepeth of which he was rector, and his son-in-law's church at Sedgefield, fitting them with stalls, screens and furniture, portions still happily spared to us. Other churches were not slow to follow the example set them, and Durham county possesses a number of examples of the furniture of this particular period. In Lancashire, Prescot was fitted with a screen and stalls in 1636. At the Restoration the church of Acton, Cheshire, was repaired, and screen and stalls of quiet and refined design placed therein. Many other churches in the country had similar work to show until the devastating period of restoration. Notable screens erected before the Commonwealth include Holdenby 1580 (219); Croscombe 1616; Tilney All Saints 1618; Stoke Rodney and Washfield 1624 and Cholmondeley 1653. Holdenby is in the heavy classic manner and is said to be the hall screen; Stoke Rodney has an unusual gallery front and Cholmondeley was ornately furnished during the Commonwealth; the others are a mixture of Netherlands, classic and strapwork designs.

The fire of London, disastrous as it was, gave a magnificent opportunity to the architects and craftsmen of that day, of which they took full advantage, and before the year 1940-1 we could study the classic revival to the full. The burnt-out cathedral was rebuilt in this style, a style originating in southern climes abounding in blue skies and sunshine, for which it was admirably fitted. The advisability of adopting it to northern climes where grey skies predominate and sunshine is the exception is more open to doubt. However the craftsmen gathered round Sir Christopher Wren; among them the best-known name is that of Grinling Gibbons; as a technical expert in woodcarving he has remained unequalled, but his inspiration was a close copy of nature, and he turned out cornucopias of work, lavish and without stint until the importance of his contribution has been undervalued. His carving and woodwork may be studied in the stallwork of St. Paul's and in many of the city churches, or rather could have been before the advent of the Nazi, for as Charles Ricketts wrote "the evil work of a fool lives after him" and his destruction of what he is incapable

220 PULPIT COVER, ST. CLEMENTS, KING WILLIAM ST., LONDON
221 FONT AND COVER, ALL HALLOWS, LOMBARD ST., LONDON

CONTINUITY OF MEDIAEVAL TRADITION IN BRASS FOUNDING

224 BRISTOL, ST. MARY REDCLIFFE
BRASS LECTERN, 1638

223 PENRITH CHURCH, CANDELABRUM, 1745

222 WELLS CATHEDRAL
BRASS LECTERN, 1670

of either understanding or doing himself is one of the tragedies of modern history. This prodigal richness of the Restoration period is the note of the time and was also found in the churches of Bristol, St. Peter's 1697; St. Thomas 1710 and Christchurch 1790; in Lancashire at St. Peter's Liverpool 1704 by Richard Prescot (now at North Meols) and at Shepton 1730. Work of this character however was but the adaptation of domestic design to ecclesiastical purposes, and was interchangeable with the dining hall of the mansion with its buttery screen, the college hall, chapel and library and the halls of the city companies; it was usable in almost any capacity, enriched and ornamented with *putti* and other emblems garnered from the outfit of the tomb-maker.

Unfortunately the nineteenth century restorer had his mild Nazi leanings and endeavoured to turn out what he did not actually destroy, so that much woodwork of the Post-reformation period has disappeared; the screen at Prescot 1636 and Bp. Hacket's stalls 1669 at Lichfield have gone, portions of the Oxford stalls have found a home at Cassington and only fragments remain of the screens at Stow-nine-churches and Middlewich; the Durham woodwork screens and pulpitum are ruined and the list could be continued.

Georgian woodwork though of sober cast was not without a certain dignity, consisting as it did of sunk panelling used in a variety of ways, but by the close of the eighteenth century church woodwork had ceased to count either in design or craftsmanship.

METALWORK IN THE SEVENTEENTH AND EIGHTEENTH CENTURIES.—After the interval of time when the smith had been employed as a locksmith the renaissance of ironwork set in, which had by the commencement of the eighteenth century produced a wealth of design and craftsmanship, a modicum finding its way into the churches; the main output however was used for the gates and railings of manorial and other mansions. Before this took place a considerable leeway had to be met, for during the charcoal period the work had been much restricted. Later however with the advent of coal these restrictions gradually disappeared. A good example of the work of the seventeenth century is the screen and railing surrounding the Warburton chapel at St. John, Chester, the screen still framed and panelled in timber, the uprights or muntins and cresting in heavily constructed ironwork, the rods twisted in the earlier manner, the cresting and protectors javelin shaped. In the railing the uprights are threaded through a wide flat cross-bar, five *fleur-de-lys* being introduced into the cresting. An early grille at Bunbury is constructed of square rods, the horizontals threaded across; here again the uprights terminate in *fleur-de-lys* alternating with javelin heads. At Farleigh Hungerford is a double gate into the side chapel made for lady Hungerford in 1650; it has four panels of "wall-anchor" pattern with a sawn iron cresting of Hungerford crests and was probably the work of the Flemings. The chancel screen at Wrexham is a mixture of styles both early and late, dating towards the close of the century; it has been suggested that the smith was Hugh Davies, father of the celebrated Robert. The churches of Bristol also show a mine of ornamental ironwork including some early sword rests (203–7).

Unfortunately the grilles around tombs have been in the majority of cases destroyed, or we might have had in sequence the history of smithing during the seventeenth century. The Oldfield monument rails 1616, in St. Mary, Chester are composed of square uprights terminating in sharpened spikes threaded through a cross-bar, the standards thickened out and completed by *fleur-de-lys*, while above are hinged banners with painted escutcheons. The rails round Bp. Dolben 1686 at York have also plain verticals connected by moulded cross-bars, the standards with twisted shafts and javelin heads resting upon ball bases; like the screen at Chester these railings are ornamented with the rose. Other classes of work included the suspension rods for the candelabra and hour-glasses stands, such as the one at Compton Bassett made from beaten plate-iron, with a domed head and enriched with *fleur-de-lys* (200).

The arrival in England of William and Mary in 1688, marked a rapid change in the format of English ironwork. Within twelve months a Frenchman named Jean Tijou arrived in this country and was fortunately introduced to the queen, whose confidence he held until her death; he was employed on the gardens at Hampton Court, making screens and other ornamental ironwork. In 1691 Wren employed him at St. Paul's; later, about 1696, he designed the quire screens and other interior fittings. These astounding elaborations were prodigal alike in design and execution, the very abundance of the enrichments defeating its own ends. Unfortunately Tijou's work like that of many another has suffered from the meddlesome interference of persons who live under the impression that they have the power to improve the original lay-out; St. Paul's offers a striking example of this deplorable want of taste. Although we know but little of the personality of Tijou, his work had a far-reaching influence upon the trend of English ironwork. Among contemporary smiths were Thomas Robinson, Partridge, Warren and George Buncker, all accomplished craftsmen whose work though less elaborate, was more dignified than that of Tijou. Robinson was employed by Wren at St. Paul's from 1697 to 1711; otherwise these craftsmen seem to have done little work in connection with churches.

Outside London, smiths were also influenced by Tijou, the more notable being Paris of Warwick, Edney of Bristol, Bakewell of Derby and Robert Davies of Wrexham, all doing important work and dividing the country between them. Of the general output of Paris more is surmised than really known. In 1716 after the fire at Warwick church he placed a new grille in front of the monument to the earl of Leicester, and was responsible for the gates and railing in the chancel placed there in 1706. His work does not show a very coherent design, but is certainly interesting. William Edney of Bristol did much church-work in his city, his screens were placed in St. Mary Redcliffe, 1710 (203–4); St. Thomas 1722, St. Nicholas and the Temple church 1726 (205–6). Here again his work has been dislodged, altered and largely spoilt. The magnificent chancel screen at Redcliffe is now at the west end, that of St. Nicholas now fences the baptistery and those at the Temple church fence the chancel from the aisles; these last form a unique collection of delicate wrought iron with many designs, decorated with acanthus foliage and medallions containing delightful monograms. Two sword rests of this date are at St. Nicholas and the Temple church; they are among the finest of their kind, especially that at St. Nicholas which is a marvellous piece of delicate design.* Robert Davies of Groes Voyle, Bersham, was responsible for some splendid ironwork, principally however gates and railings, the nearest approach to the church being the gates to the yards at Oswestry, Ruthin, Wrexham and probably Malpas, there is one exception in the iron chest at St. Asaph, covered with sheet iron, formerly used for keeping the plate. The career of Robert Bakewell of Derby was one of hardship and poverty. He made the screens for the new All Saints church, Derby in 1724, and his work has suffered much at the hands of "restorers," some of it has been unearthed in vaults and has been recently re-erected. The central overthrow of the chancel screen has an elaborate version of the "Kinges Armes"; it is suggested that he also made the screen at Staunton Harold. Other smiths produced excellent smithing such as the delightful screen at Beverley Minster, formerly the quire gates based upon a design by Tijou at Oxford; the gate into the

* Since this was written both St. Nicholas and the Temple church have been destroyed by the Nazis.

chapel at Stanton Harcourt, the grille round the font at York Minster and the screens and rails in imitation gothic in the quire of the collegiate church at Manchester. However before the close of the eighteenth century ironwork was in decline both in design and execution, and by the nineteenth century together with craftsmanship generally had reached its nadir of incompetence and wrong-headed design.

BRASS FOUNDING.—The production of lecterns of laton did not cease with the suppression; there are still four examples of the time of Archbp. Laud, Wimborne 1623, Magdalen, Oxford 1633, Exeter college, Oxford 1637, and St. Mary Redcliffe 1638 (224), the founders remaining anonymous. They however bear a strong family likeness, the shafts having renaissance vase-shaped turnings completed above by a large ball. After the Restoration, William Borroughes of London was responsible for four others, Wells 1661; Queen's, Oxford 1662; Canterbury 1663; and Lincoln 1667. In this series the design of the shaft harks back to mediaeval mouldings and stands upon small lions. These are all eagle lecterns with the exception of Wells, which is designed as a double desk and is far the finest post-Reformation lectern extant (222). Later, Jacob Sutton of London made a lectern for Salisbury in 1714; this was however sold in 1792 and is now lost. He was also responsible for the lectern at St. Paul's, made in 1720; this eagle stands upon a renaissance shaft which retains its lion's feet. The last lectern to be made was for Brazenose college, Oxford 1731, after which date the fashion and types in lecterns changed.

It was far otherwise with the candelabra, for although the earlier mediaeval and post-Reformation examples are often of foreign origin, the eighteenth century produced numberless English candelabra, and although many have been lost during misguided restorations, enough remain to show both their individuality and charm. Judging from the trade cards of the time there were many foundries, but few examples bear the names of the makers; they however were made in London, Bristol, Birmingham, Chester and other places. At Prestbury Cheshire is a good example dated 1712 with the maker's name William Davenport. This is of interest, for these Davenports are mentioned in the will of William Terry, brass founder of Chester 1728. His gifts include "to Terry Davenport sone of Mosses Davenport of the City, founder; to my kinswoman Mary, daughter of Thomas Davenport of Chester, founder and to Thomas son of Richard Davenport now living in Manchester, founder." From this it would appear that the Prestbury example was made either in Chester or Manchester; there are

two similar ones in St. John, Chester. The three-tier example at
Frodsham 1805, was made by William and Homer Silvester of
Birmingham at a cost of £50 18s. od.

The earlier types are the more elegant, the later the more
ornate. The earlier have a large ball below the lights, usually
polished to reflect the tapers. The sconces spring from the shaft
at a higher level and if of two tiers this is repeated; in the later
types however they spring from a band encircling the ball. At
first the sconces are deeply curved; later the curve becomes
shallow, interspersed with ornaments. In a later type the ball
is combined with a vase-shaped shaft, often gadrooned above
and below. The circular trays beneath the candle-holders are
at first large and shallow, later becoming cup-like. There is a
surprising variety in design, and many examples are elegant
and delightful. In construction the shaft is composed of separate
pieces held together by a central rod of iron, finishing above
with a split pin inside a loop, while below is a brass knob or
ring. The heads are decorated with doves, or later, flambeaux.
The sconces were cast, and could be interchanged for other
patterns, many of which were kept in stock, for they re-appear
again after many years. The gifts of candelabra to the churches
were continued till well into the nineteenth century; in fact
until the busy restorers began the despoliation of the churches,
robbing them of their remaining treasures.

INDEX OF ILLUSTRATIONS AND CHIEF TEXT REFERENCES

ARRANGED UNDER COUNTIES

The references in bold type are to the *figure numbers* of illustrations.

GENERAL INDEX